DUE

A movement approach
to educational gymnastics

3 γ

A movement approach to educational gymnastics

By Ruth Morison

Former Deputy Principal
I. M. Marsh College of
Physical Education
Liverpool

J M Dent and Sons Limited

ACKNOWLEDGEMENT

The author is grateful to Messrs MacDonald & Evans Ltd for permission to use a quotation from *The Mastery of Movement* by Rudolf Laban.

ISBN: 0 460 09437 8

Contents

Preface

The decision to write this book was the outcome of many requests from friends at home and abroad who have used the booklets on Educational Gymnastics written in 1956 and 1960. The present book includes a revised version of some of the material from the booklets, and a great deal of new material gathered while teaching educational gymnastics and helping students how to plan their work and carry out their teaching practice. It is intended as a textbook for students and as an aid to young teachers and to people abroad who have shown so much interest in Physical Education as it is taught in British schools today. My teaching experience has been concerned with girls and women students, but judging by the occasions when I have taught men or boys, both in Britain and abroad, I believe that this form of gymnastics has much to offer them, and the boys' work I have seen where men teachers were using this approach, achieved highly successful results.

In the preparation of the book I have had in mind the secondary school stage, but the material covers the full range of educational gymnastics and could therefore be used for primary school children. and students at college provided the teacher has the skill to modify or extend according to the understanding, experience and ability of the classes. Educational gymnastics has value in its own right, but I consider it should also be used as a means of giving experience and imparting understanding of principles which have carry-over value for other functional movement. For this reason games, athletics, swimming and daily work are often mentioned in the text. Teachers who have a sound grasp of the subject should take every opportunity of making the links apparent and of proving that all branches of movement spring from a common stem.

Preface

It would not be possible to thank individually the many people to whom I am indebted, but I should like to express my sincere thanks to Miss M. T. Crabbe, CBE, MA, for her support, encouragement and practical help, and Miss M. I. Jamieson, MA, Principal of the I. M. Marsh College of Physical Education, Liverpool, for permission to use photographs taken in the College. I am deeply grateful to Miss B. J. Lewis and Mr D. Holstead, BA (Cantab.) for planning and taking the photographs and, of course, to the students who co-operated so willingly. Indeed, I am grateful to all the students whom I taught at I. M. Marsh College, and to my former colleagues, for they have provided me with the experience from which this book has grown.

Ruth Morison

Roxburghshire 1968

Purpose and principles

MAN'S NEED FOR MOVEMENT AND THE PURPOSE OF GYMNASTICS

Man is constantly striving to prove himself in his physical environment. He no longer needs to hunt for his food, defend his home or fight for his life like his ancestors whose survival depended on skill and cunning. Yet man still values his physical powers and frequently makes for himself situations in which he pits himself against nature or his fellow men. He goes out of his way to find challenges such as mountains, potholes, unexplored regions, seas and winds, and he is willing to give his life in this quest for adventure. He also elects to compete with others in tests of speed, strength, skill and ingenuity. Most of us have some spirit of adventure, the desire to dare, the wish to have the skill and courage to deal with all sorts of physical situations, and to be confident and unafraid in matters which affect our daily lives. An innate desire to be competent and strong is expressed in many ways. People satisfy their need for skill, activity and recreation by joining athletics and sports clubs, outdoor activity groups and dance circles, and some follow radio and television Keep Fit programmes. Some even try to compensate for their inadequacies by watching and voicing their feelings about the prowess of footballers, wrestlers and boxers, and most people take a delight in seeing good, highly skilled movement whether it is the perfection of the Royal Ballet or the vivacity of the Russian National Dancers, the humorous movement of clowns or the grace and perfection of animal movement. Physical skill is an attribute highly valued for it gives great satisfaction and confidence, and contributes much to self-respect and poise.

Children's full and proper development depends on activity and includes not only physical but also social, emotional and intellectual development. Movement is a child's first mode of expression and the first means of investigating its environment. Undue limitations of movement can have serious consequences on normal development. Activity is an essential component of healthy development but not all young people get as much as they need. Their cramped environment gives too little opportunity for adventurous play so that at an early age many children develop timidities and fears which may burden them for the rest of their lives. The restrictions imposed by small homes, high flats, crowded schools, spaceless towns and the increasing supply of ready made entertainment and mechanical means of transport compel many children to quell their natural urge to move, and their inactivity tends to make them dull and passive. The result is that far too many people grow up to be physically inept. They have little confidence in their movement ability which limits their power of expression and shows in self-conscious behaviour and lack of poise. Partly through lack of sufficient activity some children are awkwardly overgrown while others are fat and flabby so that eventually desire for movement is lost and they join the ranks of the physically 'illiterate'. A good all round physical education programme in every type of school could do much to offset the existing inadequate conditions.

The school physical education programme has widened in recent years to such an extent that there is danger of losing sight of the main purpose of this branch of education. Diversity is right for giving every individual a chance to find activities which appeal, but many which have been introduced to schools are only suitable as extra-curricular activities because of the special locations needed and the amount of time required, and it would not be right to detract from the time given to routine physical education for any of these extra-curricular subjects. The curricular subjects must be those which can reasonably be part of the school timetable. The inclusion of physical education as part of the school curriculum needs no justification, but a serious question is how best to use the time allocated. This must naturally depend on the school and the facilities as well as the special gifts of the teachers in charge of the subject. It is surely more profitable for the young to get some activity as often as possible rather than have the whole allocation of time for physical education put together into one or two long periods. Of the physical education subjects offered in school, educational dance and educational gymnastics are those which most directly contribute to the personal development of children. Neither is bound by specific rules nor dependent on competition and, without loss of purpose, both can be freely adapted directly to the needs, abilities and interests of children at every stage of development.

Educational dance and gymnastics can be considered the core of movement education because through them a systematic and progressive experience of movement can be built up. Through these subjects the fundamentals of movement can be experienced and comprehended and both should, whenever possible, be part of the physical education curriculum.

Movement is universally needed for all manner of purposes. Through movement we communicate with our fellow men, and the arts of dance and drama use movement in this expressive way. It also has utilitarian purposes for getting the tasks of the day done whether they are the gross and powerful actions of manual labourers or the finer manipulations of the craftsman. The playlike forms of movement which constitute our recreational and educational activities such as ski-ing or mountaineering, games, athletics, swimming or gymnastics, all employ movement in an objective way. To be physically literate one should be creative, imaginative and clear in expressive movement, competent and efficient in utilitarian movement, and inventive, versatile and skilful in objective movement. The body is the means by which ideas and aims are carried out and, therefore, it must become both sensitive and deft.

The expressive and communicative aspect of movement can, through good teaching, be fully served by educational dance which is many-sided, satisfying both to boys and girls, adaptable to all stages of development and supplying a movement need which cannot be provided better in any other way. The functional, objective action side of movement can best be served by educational gymnastics which can be freely adapted according to the skill, spirit and needs of any group. This cannot happen in subjects such as athletics, Olympic gymnastics and various other activities which all have an unchangeable end-product and are bound by definite rules. These subjects are undoubtedly enjoyed but particularly by the physically able since measurable achievement is all important, but because of this competitive element, physically unsure people are constantly having their incompetence shown to them. This may destroy confidence and faith in any movement ability which they may have and which could be developed in other ways.

Educational gymnastics and dance complement one another but at the same time each has a unique contribution to make which is not supplied by the other. Dance has excitement and adventure of its own which is not offered by gymnastics but it does not have the kind of excitement and physical adventure provided by the use of apparatus with heights, flights and perilous moments so often

3

experienced in the agile movements of gymnastics. This is greatly enjoyed by most normal, healthy children but some of the senior girls lose interest in the robust and animal-like skill, and would rather dance. If there is no dance available, gymnastics can be adapted and made profitable and suitable for older girls. They need movement to refresh and stimulate them and many admit that, reluctant as they may be to leave their books, they feel enlivened and invigorated by a movement break. Interest in dance should never be lost for dance has something for everyone and can cater for all tastes. If a choice of dance or gymnastics could be given from about the fourth year upward, it would be ideal for this would ensure that some form of movement education is continued throughout school life.

There is common ground in the teaching of dance and gymnastics since both are based on the movement principles and ideas developed by Rudolf Laban. His work in education was with dance, but he also gave a lead in functional movement through his work in industry, and his inspiration and width of vision of movement stimulated educationists to discover for themselves the relevance of movement in other fields. Many pioneers started to experiment and look in his way and this has brought about a radical change in physical education in Britain.

At an elementary level dance and gymnastics lessons may appear to start in much the same way. Both begin with some type of movement experience through which people learn to move the body as a unit, discover many ways of moving and various qualities of movement, feel changes of tension, use different speeds and directions and experiment with moving and stopping. The similarities are, however, superficial because the stimuli which evoke movement in each situation are different. In dance lessons the stimuli touch the imagination, and teacher and class together create an atmosphere in which dance can flourish and in which the movement has dance-like quality. The gymnastic stimuli are concerned with objects which have to be used or with the body itself manipulated as an object to be bent, stretched and twisted, thrown in the air and caught again, and an energetic, lively and inventive atmosphere should prevail. The intention in the two situations is basically different. The reason for moving in gymnastics and all functional movement is to do something objective, while in dance and allied arts it is to express something through movement. Expressive movement is the visible manifestation of moods, feelings and ideas which can be communicated to other people. Functional movement on the

4

other hand, primarily has an external focus and deals with objects to be handled or practical tasks to be done, and attention and action are directed to those ends.

Educational purpose of gymnastics

Children need adventure, fun and an opportunity to move energetically. To the city child and the over-protected child of our welfare state, a modern gymnasium can provide some scope for adventurous playlike activity and plenty of fun. It offers a variety of challenges and enables people to discover themselves and their potentialities in this field of movement. They are helped to experience and understand movement in order to become agile and skilful and they learn to handle a variety of objects with confidence. They also have opportunity to work with others by helping, sharing and co-operating. They learn to assess their own ability, and gain control and confidence from their experience and from the encouragement and appreciation which they are given by their teacher and contemporaries. The teaching of educational gymnastics is comparable with certain aspects of the teaching of art in that everyone is set to work in an individual way, results are only compared as interesting contrasts and everyone's efforts are studied and criticised as a contribution to the learning process.

An important purpose in educational gymnastics is to develop each individual's latent movement powers as far as possible. Those who have the greatest need of movement education are the clumsy, incompetent and timid, and they also need the most encouragement and help. Physical inadequacy and fear can be devastating and competition is, therefore, out of place as it will provide an unfortunate stimulus and simply discourage and frustrate people when they are challenged beyond their powers and compared with their more able contemporaries. Competition is inherent in games, athletics and many other activities and those who particularly enjoy it get it in these subjects, but it is also a salutary discipline for these same people to learn to control a competitive attitude and to discover the interest and satisfaction of working without always striving to be first or best. There are many teachers who argue that because life is competitive, it is an education to face it, but faith in one's own movement ability is so important that to take this from the weaker ones can have an adverse effect for life. Physical ineptitude can hold people back, hinder their development, and prevent them even attempting things they would like to do. One realises how much normal movement matters when one sees the prodigious efforts made by those with physical defects to overcome their disabilities. Since skill is a matter of degree, teachers should do all in their power to give people a belief in their possibilities. Many of the less gifted quickly gain confidence when they realise they are allowed to choose their own way of doing things and work in their own time. They must also feel accepted and be given a full share of help and encouragement. Some need to be convinced that there are many ways of tackling problems and that it is their approach to the problems and their ways of resolving them which are of value rather than the end result. When this is accepted courage and interest grow.

There are very few pre-constructed exercises in this form of gymnastics because all individuals have personal ways of moving which should be developed, and they should be encouraged to invent their own patterns of movement based on the problems prescribed by the teacher. One often describes people as lively, impulsive, tentative, calm, direct and so on. One may be thinking of traits of character and personality but the same qualities describe movement characteristics which are an integral part of the individual. The teacher of movement takes into account all such personal differences within a class as well as recognising the varying stages of development and rates and ways of learning. People should first be helped to recognise their own strengths and the starting point is always what an individual can do. Those who are quick and lively have gifts in this direction, while those who are slow and careful excel when such movement is needed. Through recognition of such differences a teacher can start to build up an appreciation and understanding of the value of every kind of movement. As confidence grows and skill increases everyone should come to grips with and master all types of movement; much latent talent is there waiting to be developed by the teacher who can uncover it.

An exploratory approach to new work should be used at all stages for tasks can be devised to satisfy the advanced as well as the beginners. The teaching of techniques should follow exploration and they are introduced, as needed, to improve movement and to counteract harmful habits. Techniques may sometimes be used to help in the mastery of simple skills which form the foundation for more complex ones, but the teacher should be careful not to impose too many specific skills as this could create the impression that these skills have more value than those invented by the youngsters themselves. If this happens they may lose their initiative and desire to be inventive and come to rely passively on the teacher for ideas.

However, this does not mean that the teacher is passive, for alertness to the need for help is imperative as well as to the moment when help should be given. Helping *is* teaching and cannot be confused with imposing if the aims of fostering creativeness, innate ability and confidence are always kept in mind. Teaching and working in this way make heavy demands; teachers must be observant, perceptive and alert, always ready to help and encourage, able to judge, assess, think and take action; children will be kept attentive and absorbed by a good choice of work, and they will be called upon to make decisions and to act upon them. Inventive powers are brought into play and perseverance is tested where the attainment of skill stretches each one to the limits. Children are also expected to be observant and considerate, and all these things depend on a sense of responsibility and a feeling for self-discipline. When working in this way every aspect of the human being is integrated for body, will and mind all have a part to play.

Physical purpose of gymnastics

It goes without saying that the educational and the physical aspects are inter-dependent, but there has been a tendency in recent times to play down and even ignore the physical effects. This is short-sighted and unwise. Observant and responsible teachers are concerned about the general well-being, health and sound development of those in their care, and this includes physical development. A well planned, regular gymnastics course should have a beneficial effect on physique and promote general fitness. A properly conducted lesson will give a great deal of strenuous exercise and stimulate the whole body because gymnastic actions consist mainly of large movements using all the big muscle groups. The alternate contraction and relaxation involved in muscular movement has a pumping effect and in most gymnastic actions the whole body contracts and squeezes, releases and extends, in greater or lesser degree, and this constant alteration of pressure stirs and stimulates all the organs and tissues of the body.

It is also important that the normal mobility of the body should be safeguarded and this depends on the state of the muscles and tissues around joints. Joints should be moved to their limits, without straining, to keep the right muscular balance around them. Full stretching and pulling outward away from the centre of the body has a tonic and prophylactic effect. Animals limber by stretching after resting, and it might prove a sound practice to follow their example. Teachers could encourage people to stretch fully several times during the school day and so help to stave off the stiffness and awkwardness to which all are prone if they fail to get as much activity as they need.

The Swedish system of gymnastics consisted of a series of exercises for each part of the body in turn so that all joints were used in full range and all muscles systematically exercised. Our educational gymnastics, based on movement principles, should also ensure all round activity, but unless the teacher is aware of this need and plans the lesson with it in mind, and watches the youngsters as they work, it is quite possible for many children to avoid certain very necessary corrective movements. The structure of the lesson, as suggested in this book, takes into account the need for all round balanced activity. The joints and muscles of the limbs are well catered for particularly in the apparatus work; hanging and swinging, and actions with weight on arms use the arms and shoulder girdle, but they must be used correctly. In jumping and vaulting the legs are used strongly but the teaching in flight and landing must be sound for the work to be fully effective. But unless careful attention is given to actions using movements of the spine and trunk so that they are deliberately used and fully twisted, arched, bent and stretched to the limits, in every lesson, this vital part of the body can escape from going through the range of movement which is needed to keep it pliable, resilient and strong. The hips should also be activated in conjunction with movements of the trunk because they are not often used in full range in daily life or in many physical education activities and, all too easily, they appear to stiffen up and become limited in range. In children the limitations are more likely to be caused by inability to make the neuro-muscular connection which vitalises the muscles acting on the joints, rather than any real stiffness. Frequent and conscious use develops kinaesthetic feeling in the region and increases range of movement. An awareness of the relationship of the hips and pelvis to movements of the trunk and legs must also be developed.

Understanding and feeling for movement can also affect the carriage of the body and growing kinaesthetic awareness can help to counteract bad postural habits and establish good ones. There are many occasions in a lesson where the carriage of the body needs to be stressed for full effectiveness in action. Starting and finishing positions, as well as the way the body is carried and held while moving, influence the whole execution of actions. At the same time, plenty of varied, active movement is necessary to develop and balance the musculature and keep the body limber; good muscular control and lack of stiffness, both contribute to lithe and graceful carriage. The causes of mal-development and poor carriage are legion, but unless the faults are structural, physical education teachers have power to combat them through their teaching. There are plenty of opportunities to observe the physique of the children and many minor faults can be detected and corrected at the school stage of life which, if ignored, may cause trouble later. Physical means alone, however, will not have the desired effect because many other factors affect the poise and carriage of the body, and these must also be taken into account as they are probably of even greater importance. Temperament, confidence, sense of security, current attitudes and fashions affect the way people hold themselves and are also reflected in the way they move. Physical education teachers who are aware of these things can do a great deal to foster interest in the problem and give encouragement to young people in this matter which is so vital to them. They can also help to mould the attitude of their colleagues and the children's parents through interest, enthusiasm and example.

The limitations imposed by contemporary life tend to disrupt natural harmonious movement and produce stilted, restricted, isolated actions, and to develop bad habits of movement and carriage which in their turn cause tensions, cramps and the resultant ills. It is, therefore, urgent to help people to understand how to use the body effectively. Movement which stresses awareness of all parts of the body and the interaction of various parts with one another is part of every lesson. Use of the body as a unit should always be stressed since economy and grace depend on whole body participation in action. The grace, ease and perfect rightness which is so evident in animal movement is also possible for the human being, for man, being an animal, has the innate capacity for harmonious movement. Effective use of the body is experienced in many gymnastic situations which are closely allied to the utilitarian movement for everyday tasks. Gymnastics entails the handling of various objects by grasping, lifting, carrying, placing, pushing, pulling, and the principles for doing these things should be made clear and experienced. General body management, which is needed for ordinary living, is developed through actions which improve body balance, agility in moving about, nimbleness in getting up and down, and reaching and stretching in all directions. Teachers must help by drawing attention to the similarities of movement in and out of the gymnasium.

Conclusion

The purpose of educational gymnastics is to produce good movers who have had a wide and general experience of movement and who understand its use for many purposes. We hope that people who have had a thorough training will be 'masters of movement' and, therefore, will be able to approach all types of movement with greater understanding and well prepared bodies. A good physical education teacher will arouse interest in the significance of movement generally and will help people to understand that the experience gained through their movement education provides another source of appreciation and awareness of their whole environment. A good teacher will also succeed in convincing everyone that each has something to give and that everyone matters. Some of the physically less able can contribute much by their good observation, constructive criticism and generous help. Many of the academically less able come into their own in gymnastics lessons. They are often physically able and hard working and thrive on encouragement; they can be most sensible and willing helpers. It undoubtedly gives them strength and confidence to realise their success and their obvious ability to contribute.

The more general educational purposes depend very greatly on the climate in the school as well as on the attitude of the teacher. There is much more likely to be a carry over from the gymnasium if this same atmosphere permeates the school. One of the chief educational purposes of gymnastics is to develop awareness, not only of the body and the effect of movement, but of the whole environment, and this includes the people in it. Growth of general awareness depends on the teacher and the relationship and atmosphere between teacher and children. A belief in the value of giving children freedom, a chance to choose and find out for themselves, to make mistakes, to take decisions and come to conclusions, is essential. Such beliefs are the negation of trust in the effectiveness of rules, dogma and imposed disciplines, and it takes a great deal of courage for a young and inexperienced teacher to go through with such convictions. It is sometimes difficult to know how to be firm without being tyrannical, and how to keep the respect due to authority and yet to listen and be considerate of the children's point of view, but these things, together with kindness and constancy are vital in a robust subject like gymnastics in which it would be easy to become domineering and harsh.

PRINCIPLES AND ANALYSIS OF FUNCTIONAL MOVEMENT

All movement has common factors. There is always a 'thing' which moves or is moved, and something to make it move. In the human being the 'thing' is the body and the forces which make it move are gravity or other external forces, various stimuli which make us act reflexly or consciously, and our own will and other personal driving forces. Rudolf Laban called these personal driving forces Efforts and he described them as 'inner impulses from which movement originates'. 'Inner impulse' implies the use of the will or the mind to induce and control action of the body. This body-mind relationship is a profound psychological study of movement and quite beyond the scope or needs of a book on gymnastics. Nevertheless, even without full understanding of the psychological aspects of movement, a knowledge of the way the components of motion (Time, Weight, Space and Flow) are blended to give various dynamic qualities of movement is of inestimable value in the teaching, analysis and observation of functional movement.

The four factors of movement are always blended in action. Every movement takes a quantity of time and energy (Weight), space is used, and the movement flows from start to finish. When a human being moves, because thought, will and feelings as well as the body are engaged, movement takes on another dimension, that of quality as well as quantity. Our human make-up gives each one of us our own individual characteristics, and according to the way we feel and think so our movement and behaviour are determined. Some people show dynamic energy in all they do, while others have a more leisurely approach to life. In recognising such characteristics one is seeing the quality of people's movement rather than the measurable aspects of it. Generally speaking, people's natural characteristics predispose them to certain types of movement which they find easier and more part of themselves, and in teaching movement this must be taken into account. As teachers, we should first try to make everyone confident and secure through their own greatest gifts, and gradually lead them to a wider variety of movement. This does not mean that at first slow movers should only move slowly, or quick ones quickly. We should demand all kinds of movement from everyone, according to their ability, but the quick, slow, gentle, forceful, direct or flexible movers should each gain recognition of their particular talents. This is, to a point, easier in dance teaching, because in gymnastics, where movement has an objective purpose, there is less choice of the way in which certain tasks can be tackled because they are subject to mechanical laws. To jump on to a swinging rope, or to catch and balance a partner, leaves only a little choice for the quality of movement which can be used. The right amount of force must be used, the speed, timing and direction are predetermined and must be assessed and produced to make the action effective. It is mainly such quantitative aspects of movement which are stressed in teaching gymnastics and other functional activities. Nevertheless, good teachers have always taken into account the personality and individuality of the people they teach. They select work which is suitable for the class and they welcome the personal interpretation of any task and the individual quality shown in the actions created by the children.

Most people move and do all sorts of tasks without any technical knowledge of movement, and those who are innate good movers will manage better than others who are not so gifted. Experience of movement and a growing awareness and understanding gives people an extra 'tool' with which they can help themselves and it is the means by which they can 'learn to learn'. A teacher who understands the basic principles of movement and who can think and observe in a movement way, is better able to help people to tackle the tasks confronting them, and so enable them to do as they wish, in the way they wish. Through encouraging this personal and individual way, people gain skill and progress is made.

In analysing any action, swimming, athletics, games skills as well as gymnastics, there are three main considerations:

> The body   i e *what* the body is doing
>
> Movement   i e *how* the body is being moved
>
> Space   i e *where* the movement is going

The body

The bodily aspect of action is concerned with *what* the body is doing. There are two main points to observe:
> The parts of the body which support the weight (the base), held as in standing on one leg, or transitorily as in rolling.
> The parts of the body which are not supporting weight and which can, therefore, move in space.

Body support (*the base*)

Most parts of the body can support the body weight and many of the traditional skills come from balancing the weight on surfaces of the body such as the head, hands or forearms, and children find many other parts which can bear their weight. Sometimes several parts may be used, matching parts such as both shoulders, both hips or knees, or non-matching parts such as one hand and one knee, or one forearm and one shoulder.

The body weight may also pass transitorily over various surfaces of the body as in rocking or rolling and in other ways of transferring weight including all forms of locomotion and flight.

Body movement in space

The parts of the body which are free to move (because they are not supporting weight) can bend, stretch and twist. These movements bring about weight transference which results in all forms of locomotion, or they may be non-locomotory where movement is confined within the personal sphere of space.

Movement

This aspect of motion is concerned with *how* the body is moved, with the dynamic aspect of action which gives quality to movement and includes rhythm and timing, speed and tension changes and the fluctuations in the flow of movement. The four motion factors are Time, Weight, Space and Flow. These are the ingredients of all movement, and though in teaching movement it is possible to isolate and concentrate attention on a single factor to the exclusion of the rest, in action, elements of all factors are blended together and they cannot be divorced. The four factors of motion are described separately for the sake of clarity.

The Time factor

The Time Factor is concerned with speed of motion and the amount of time used in an action. A single movement can be lightning quick or infinitely slow or scaled between these two extremes. Actions are nearly always built up of movements of varying speed, and in a vigorous vault the run is accelerated to give the necessary momentum for the take-off which is a very quick, strong movement, while the speed of the flight depends on the type of vault. Never, in natural movement is the speed quite uniform, it fluctuates according to the needs of the action.

The sensations of suddenness and lingering which are associated with quick and slow actions give quality to movement. For example, in making a cartwheel, the performer may enjoy lingering over it and prolonging the action, or in a jump, the body shape which can be assumed in the flight may be sustained and held until the last moment, and then be suddenly released a split second before landing. This non-mechanical and non-measurable side of movement is what gives it quality and it depends on the performer's personal interpretation and control of action.

The Weight factor

The Weight Factor relates to energy output and the effect this has in producing various degrees of muscular tension for the execution of movement. This is the factor of motion which is most intimately bound up with the body itself, since in order to move, changes have to be made within it. We have the ability to make ourselves feel light and move with lightness, or feel strong and move with strength, or we can move with other qualities such as heaviness or elasticity. These changes can partly be described in terms of degrees of muscular tension but this only gives a small part of the picture as there are many physiological changes with every muscular exertion. The changes are also consciously or subconsciously determined. One cannot be firm without willing it, or light and resilient without feeling buoyant or bouncy, and it is this awareness which gives quality to movement.

Strong movement demands considerable muscular tension and firmness of mind and body, whereas light movement needs much less tension. Strength is most naturally associated with movement towards the ground and with the powerful and muscular lower parts of the body. In strong movement there is generally great tension and firmness in the hips, thighs, legs and the pelvis as in all strong pushing, pulling, gripping, thrusting, punching or hitting movements. Lightness, on the other hand, belongs more to the buoyant upper parts, to the arms and chest, and the sensation of lightness is intensified by associating it with breathing, with inhalation. Light movement feels more peripheral and it tends to rise into the air, and there is only a slight sensation of any muscular tension.

The degree of strength used depends on the resistance which has to be overcome, so for example, in a pushing contest with a partner, or in climbing a rope, much muscular power is exerted, but in steadying a partner balanced in a headstand, only the lightest touch should be necessary. A firm position which might be needed for catching the full weight of a partner, depends on great energy generated and held in the body, but in a firm action, such as thrusting the whole weight of the body away from the ground and high into the air, the energy is released to act upon the resistance of the body weight. Lightness can also be experienced both in holding positions (lightly poised) or in actions which ask for a light touch, such as light contacting of apparatus while crossing it.

Heavy movement is the result of relaxing and releasing nearly all tension. Swinging movements depend on the dead weight of the swinging part, and this is the main type of movement which needs heaviness. Heaviness is a passive state, giving way to the physical weight of the body, whereas strength and lightness are active states demanding mental exertion. We want a minimum of passive heaviness in gymnastics and teachers should do all in their power to help people to master themselves and be able to command the built-in power of the body.

The Space factor

The Space Factor has less to do with our space environment than with our attitude to space and the influence this has on the way we move. Movement can be made with a feeling of directness, of restriction and straightness, which results in an economical use of space, or it can be made with a feeling of flexibility and freedom which produces roundabout, wavy bodily gestures and a generous use of space. These two contrasting sensations lead to quite different ways of moving and each gives a specific quality to movement. Movement in gymnastics tends to be direct but there is a place for flexibility as in twirling, turning jumps and vaults or weight transferences with twisting, turning and many changes of direction.

The Flow factor

Flow describes the actual 'going' of movement and is the unifying factor of motion. Flow of movement brings about the union of separate parts of actions, giving wholeness, rhythm and fluency. The flow of movement may be bound, that is, restrained and controlled so that it can readily be stopped. Movement which is free flowing, unrestrained and abandoned, occurs less in gymnastics where control of motion is so important, but one does sometimes launch off-balance and fly wildly through the air, allowing the movement to go and take its own course. This aspect of movement can be and also should be enjoyed in gymnastics. Movement may also be continuous or broken. Continuous movement often gives smoothness and fluency since there is no stop or interruption. Broken movement is caused by arresting and holding movement in check at one or more points in the course of an action.

The flow of movement through space starts when the body is unbalanced and travels in space, and it is checked when the body regains balance and stops travelling. The flow of movement through the body itself occurs when the body is bent, stretched or twisted. Movement flows to and from and through the centre of the body, and round or across the personal space surrounding the body.

Space aspects of action

This is concerned with the orientation of movement in space. The body itself occupies space and it is surrounded by space, i e the Personal Space. The outer limits of this space are reached by extending in all directions, up, down, forward, backward and sideways and in all intermediate directions, and at all levels, high, medium and low without altering the base. Movement can take place in the personal space near or far from the body, towards or away from it or peripherally round about it. This occurs in all movements of bending, stretching and twisting. The personal space is surrounded by the General Space which is bounded by the physical limits of the environment. Movement can take place in this space in all directions and through all levels as when travelling low near the floor and leaping high into the air. While moving in the general space a pathway is traced on the floor, the Floor Pattern, and this has an influence on movement. Certain movements, e g 100 yards sprint or hurdling are more successful if the pathway is dead straight, but other movements such as dodging in and out of people, follow a more wavy, twisty pathway. The Air Patterns which are formed by moving parts of the body have more significance in dance but in gymnastics they are a by-product of movement. There are times, however, when it may be helpful to clarify the air pattern, for example to point out the course of the body through the air in diving on to the hands, or in the curved patterns of turning movements.

Background to educational gymnastics

This brief, outline sketch gives the principles upon which gymnastic movement is based and the next section gives a picture of educational gymnastics and how the principles are used in practice. Rudolf Laban did not himself evolve any form of gymnastics but he made it quite clear that this way of approaching movement is valid in every form of human movement. Because of the outstanding quality of his thought and work in fields in which he had developed his ideas (Theatre, Education, Recreation and Industry) he inspired people in education to think and wonder about the type of work they were doing, and about the principles which had been accepted since Physical Education became a part of the school curriculum. This then was one beginning of a radical re-thinking about movement by teachers of physical education, and when eventually gymnastics based on these lines started to develop, Laban showed interest, gave encouragement and approval to the first tentative steps.

It was first necessary to put aside one's training in gymnastics in order to become free and to look afresh. It was important to rediscover how people move by the light of nature. The publication of the Ministry of Education, *Moving and Growing* proved a great inspiration in guiding people's looking and thinking towards the children themselves, how they move and what they do, and what they are capable of at each stage of development. It led teachers into wishing to and having the courage to experiment for themselves. By exchanging experience with others, meeting and working together at courses, and through the development of ideas which spring to life at teachers' centres, in Colleges of Physical Education and Colleges of Education, the present Educational Gymnastics evolved.

The development of the subject shown in this book is one interpretation. There are, and always will be others because all teachers should think and develop their work in a personal way, according to their own strengths, their conditions and the needs of their classes. But everything must be based on a sound foundation and for this, teachers of gymnastics need basic background knowledge of:

The growth and development of children.

Educational principles including child psychology.

Anatomy for understanding the structure of the body and why it can move as it does.

Physiology for understanding the essentials of how movement comes about and the effect of movement on the body.

Kinesiology for understanding the mechanical principles of movement.

and a deeper study of:

> The Art of movement including:
>
> > Movement observation which is the key to creative and educational ways of teaching.
> >
> > Movement study of:
> >
> > > Bodily action
> > >
> > > Effort
> > >
> > > Choreutics
> > >
> > > > through:
> > >
> > > Personal practice and exploration
> > >
> > > Observation
> > >
> > > Kinetography, particularly Motif writing which enables teachers to record movement.

All these subjects are matters for specialists and the practising teacher can only have a bare outline knowledge in so many different fields. Practising teachers are in the same position as general practitioners who must rely on the superior knowledge and findings in the research of the specialists. The practitioners constantly go to the specialists for help and advice. The specialists in our profession will also willingly give guidance and inspiration which is always sought and needed by progressive teachers.

The material of gymnastics

THE NATURAL MOVEMENT OF CHILDREN

The material of educational gymnastics is largely drawn from the natural everyday activities of children. Energetic, normal children like to rush about, turn upside down and turn cartwheels, hop, jump, skip, climb, swing, balance, push, pull, wrestle, and test their skill in many other ways. Children can be seen in the parks, playgrounds and streets, turning somersaults round safety rails, climbing on to 'bus shelters and jumping down, balancing on railings, swinging and climbing on lamp posts and trees, rolling and sliding down steep banks, chasing each other and throwing themselves about in sheer exuberance of spirits. Educational gymnastics profits by these interests and should make use of this skill-forming movement, extending the range of it, developing and refining it, and through it helping people to master their movement and become skilful as well as more resourceful and courageous.

All the activities described above develop general ability to manage the body and to control the body weight and this is a major consideration if people are to become nimble and agile. Given opportunity, children can go far in this way without help or instruction, but good teaching can lead people, through movement experience, to a much wider and deeper understanding. People get great satisfaction from learning how to become more versatile and skilful and from knowing they are masters in many different situations. The range of activity is extended and versatility increased by the way the work is presented and developed. The material is generally presented in the form of problems to be solved or tasks to be carried out, by every one in his own way. Youngsters are taught how to explore and experiment and in this way they increase the range of what they are doing: they gain general skill and versatility through this experience. They also learn by seeing the efforts of others both while working with partners and through short sessions of observing movement with the teacher, and in this way they gain a wider vision of the possibilities of movement. The quantity of apparatus in a good gymnasium gives opportunity for many adventurous undertakings such as swinging and climbing to great heights, jumping, balancing, turning upside down, tumbling and rolling, and people are taught to handle everything deftly.

There is also need to refine and master the skills discovered and invented. When youngsters have reached the first stage of managing their weight in a general way, the next step is to improve the quality of movement and to gain greater precision and accuracy, and this depends on three factors of equal importance:

> The bodily aspect of action which means the movements of the body itself, bending, stretching and twisting which bring about action and give form.

> The dynamic aspect of action which gives quality to movement, and this is connected with rhythm and control of the flow of movement.

> The spatial aspects of action which determine the directions, levels and extensions in movement and, therefore, give accuracy.

Educational gymnastics is built around all these natural activities and the various aspects of movement which bring skill and refinement to action. The material, therefore, comprises:

General management of the body in:

> Actions emphasising locomotion:
>> Transference of weight.
>> Travelling.
>> Flight.

> Actions emphasising balance:
>> Weight bearing.
>> Balancing skills.
>> Actions of 'arriving'.
>> On- and Off-balance.

Specific control of movement in:

> Bodily aspects of action.
> Dynamic aspects of action.
> Spatial aspects of action.

Handling

Relationships

i e Partner and Group work.

Understanding of the material

The material in Part II is described in a way which gives an over-all picture of what is involved in each aspect of gymnastics and this means that it cannot be used, as it stands, as themes for lessons, for all stages from elementary to advanced, are described under each heading. Teachers must, therefore, make their own selection from the material according to the needs of their classes. This is always essential since classes, even of the same age and in the same school, differ so greatly. For this reason no hypothetical lesson plans, nor imaginary development of themes, nor wording of tasks are given in this book except the few examples which are used as guidance to illustrate the principles involved. From the beginning inexperienced teachers should learn how to think out and plan their own lessons without relying on second-hand, ready made ideas, and discerning teachers, who understand their subject, always like to arrange their own work appropriately for their classes, conditions and themselves, and this is essential if teaching is to be individual, sensitive and apt.

The truest and soundest way to gain knowledge of the subject is through personal practical experience and this is the only way to gain depth of understanding and feeling for the matter. Practical work also gives people insight into the processes of learning and gaining skill, and they need this too if they are to be sympathetic to the problems of children's learning. The real knowledge which comes from practice, helps teachers to be better able to select and assess their lesson material wisely.

Theory and reading about movement are always more revealing and stimulating if the subject matter is translated into action. Movement is never adequately expressed in words nor grasped through the intellect; words and thinking take on new meaning by being converted into action and it is always important to try to experience in reality what words are attempting to convey. Practical experience backed up by theoretical knowledge is a step towards sound teaching, but in the actual teaching situation, the added ability to observe movement accurately, which is also gained through practical work, is the key to knowledge of what is needed and how to proceed.

The detail given in some of the descriptions which follow is to give the teacher an insight into what is involved in the subject, but it is not meant to be presented to the children in this way unless it happens to be exactly suitable. Teachers must be fully conversant with the principles underlying their subject and all the detail connected with it but they must be most discriminating about what they select to teach and when they choose to teach it. This must be strictly related to the skill, interest, response and understanding of those being taught, so that spontaneity and enjoyment are kept alive.

ACTIONS EMPHASISING LOCOMOTION

TRANSFERENCE OF WEIGHT

Transference of weight occurs in all forms of locomotion including Flight, and is used in Balancing Skills when the weight is moved from one balance position to another. The weight-bearing parts of the body are those which touch the ground (or apparatus) to support the weight.

Transference of weight is an important aspect of bodily management in which the purpose is to transfer the weight on to or over various surfaces of the body. In teaching this material one purpose is to develop awareness of the parts of the body which touch the ground and support the weight; pressure on these parts is easily felt. Another stress is concerned with what the rest of the body is doing (bodily aspect of action) and how it is moving (dynamic aspect of action) to allow the performer's intention to be carried out. The material covers much groundwork which is essential for safety and control in gymnastics.

Transference of weight is specifically stressed in certain skills:
Rocking and Rolling in which the weight is generally transferred over regions of the trunk.

'Step-like' actions in which mainly the limbs are used for supporting the weight.

Rocking and rolling

Many of these actions entail rolling on the back and whenever possible mats should be used. Thin children should not be asked to roll on a bare floor as they can hurt and severely bruise their spines. If rolling on the floor is done voluntarily as part of an action, it is a different matter, it would be unlikely then to be hurtful.

In order to rock or roll the weight must be transferred on *rounded* surfaces. Youngsters should experience how to round themselves in different positions so that they can rock or roll smoothly, without jarring or bumping. Children enjoy tasks of finding out which parts of their bodies will make 'rockers' and they will probably try rocking on their feet, seats and shoulders as well as all parts of the trunk. They will discover that they can rock on their fronts or backs (lengthwise or across), their sides and also obliquely across the body, as from one shoulder to the opposite hip, and they should feel what difference it makes if the rocker is long or short. In teaching, the holding of a good body shape must be stressed and this depends on the skilful management of muscular tension. These factors are necessary to ensure that the rocking is continuous and smooth, and without bumps. Through such experience children learn much about managing and directing their weight where they wish it to go.

Bumpy rocking and rolling is generally due to stiffness of the spine or inco-ordination. The actions have a good corrective effect if a special effort is made to round out the flat parts. In rocking on the back, stiffness of the lower back is often revealed, but many backs are corrected by a pelvic movement of tucking the 'tail' in as the backward rocking starts. This has the effect of rounding the lower end of the spine. In rocking on the front some children exaggerate the movement in the lumbar region and they should be encouraged to move right through the spine and to make a special effort to extend the dorsal spine. The pelvis should always move as part of the spine, decreasing tilt with flexion, increasing tilt with extension and tilting sideways with lateral movements. In daily life the pelvis is often held too still and this results in stiffness of the lumbar spine which in turn affects the whole spine.

As a result of experimenting and discovering many ways of rocking, more difficult skills can be evolved. If the rocking is increased there comes a moment when it is possible to rock up to the point of balance and hold the weight poised over one or other end of the rocker. A sensation of swinging up towards this point can be enjoyed by getting almost to the point of balance before tumbling back in the reverse direction. Movement sequences can be built up in which the rocking grows, nearer and nearer to the point of balance, finally to arrest the rocking and hold the body poised. Such skills need good feeling for body shape and ability to control the muscular grip of the body, particularly to hold it balanced over the base, and to control the speed by not letting go suddenly when re-starting the rocking. Some people may discover how to turn over and continue rocking on another surface. This needs good timing and ability to twist quickly and firmly. The class can be given the task of discovering how to turn over without interrupting the rocking. They must twist the raised end of the rocker, and the twist must be powerful and quick enough to turn a new surface to face the floor, before the body falls; as it falls it will turn over. Quick, skilful muscular adjustments must be made so that the body shape will allow the rocking to continue.

Rolling

Some children are, at first, afraid of rolling so it should be carefully introduced for the sake of the few. Beginners should be encouraged to find out for themselves several ways of rolling. Many children believe that 'head over heels' is expected of them so it should be made clear, at once, that this is only one way of rolling and that there are many equally good ways. The teacher can help the timid ones by getting them to start low on the floor, lying stretched out or curled up, and then they roll by tipping over sideways to turn over and over along the length of the mattress. As they become skilled in this simple way they generally gain confidence and become more adventurous. Having discovered many ways of rolling and the different regions on which they can roll, youngsters can experiment with ways of changing shape and direction as they go. They should feel what it is like to travel at various speeds and discover the ways in which they personally can roll most easily, and then practise some of these ways until they become really expert. This training is valuable as a safety measure, for children will resort to rolling when they fall if they are skilful and confident in it. Symmetrical rolls are not the most suitable for everyone; sideways rolls or other asymmetrical rolls are easier for many and definitely to be advocated for anyone with a very long or stiff back, in order to avoid strain. Youngsters must be taught to protect their heads and limbs; elbows and knees must be kept off the floor when rolling in an extended shape, and while they are inexpert, if rolling in a ball shape, it is safer to stay tightly curled up, with the head tucked in. Those who do not keep a firm grip of the body, tend to open out when rolling fast, and then the weight of the head causes it to be left behind and this may result in jerking the neck.

Both the bodily and dynamic aspects of action should be stressed in rocking and rolling. The teacher must see that the children understand the importance of holding the body in rounded shapes, and this needs the ability to regulate muscular tension. Rocking and rolling actions have significant secondary effects because they give strong muscular work to the trunk and they have a mobilising and corrective effect on the spine. The actions can bring about full bending, stretching, arching and twisting which all help to make and keep the body lithe, therefore, from a physical point of view, this type of action is worth including in every lesson.

Step-like Actions

Whereas rocking and rolling stress mainly the use of the trunk for weight bearing, the step-like actions make more use of the limbs, although one can 'step' on to many parts of the body. A step consists of:

> a 'gesture' to move the receiving part into position,
>
> placing the part,
>
> moving the weight on to or over the part.

This is clearly illustrated in Balancing actions. One 'steps' into position; the receiving part, e g the shoulder region, moves towards a place, it is placed, then the weight is moved so that the centre of gravity arrives vertically over the supporting part. Big, resilient walking steps also show the three parts clearly—gesture, placing and weight transference.

There are several 'step-like' actions with slightly different stresses:

Receiving the weight

(Mats should generally be used because these actions often include rolling.) Practice in receiving the weight on to different parts of the body is an aid to safety. Experiments can be made of lowering the body to make various parts of it touch the ground first. As soon as the chosen part touches, the whole body should yield gently so that the weight is transferred on to and over the part, to start a rocking or rolling action. Hips, thighs, knees, shoulders, the back of the neck, one elbow, one forearm, one or both hands can all touch first, but not the head because of danger to the neck. To prove control the part should touch lightly before taking the weight (page 116), and until the trunk touches, the inexperienced should try to move slowly. The scope of the action can be widened by starting in various relationships to the mat, sideways, facing or back to it, and the lowering can be straight down or with twisting. By twisting, the situation becomes less predictable and greater adaptability is needed because it is not easy to know exactly which part will touch first. The rocking or rolling should eventually be followed by a recovery on to the feet so that the sequence of lowering, touching, rocking or rolling, and recovery make a complete phrase. Elasticity, strength and resilience of legs and body are developed by practices of coming out of a roll and up on to the feet. The main ways in which this is done is through walking, running, or springing out of the roll. When the feet check the rolling by touching the ground, the body has considerable momentum from the roll which carries the weight upwards until the body is nearly extended, but some effort must be added to extend the knees fully, to stretch the spine and lift the head so that the action is terminated with upright poised carriage. Unless the teacher draws attention to the need to stretch the knees and extend the body, many children will move away from the roll in a semi-stretched position without any awareness of how to take hold of the body to lift it and carry it with poise. Properly done this action is most valuable for strengthening the legs and developing all the extensor muscle groups which play so great a part in the carriage of the body. It is much less strenuous and exacting, when jumping from a height, to roll after landing, and heavy children and others with feeble legs, soon learn the knack of rolling and springing up, and so have much less difficulty in landing without jarring or hurting themselves.

At a more advanced stage these actions can be greatly speeded up. The lowering can be very fast, with only a momentary check before touching and rolling. As skill increases, the mat can be approached by walking, running, jumping or spinning towards it, lowering and 'throwing' the weight over various parts to roll and recover. Obviously this should only be attempted by people who can manage many types of rolling, who can keep a grip of themselves to hold a rounded shape, and they must know how to protect all parts of themselves. Accurate timing is needed for the recovery on to the feet when rolling at high speed. If the moment of opening out is mistimed, balance will be lost. This type of work, together with other types of landing described in the section on Flight (page 44), can be used in the floorwork to prepare for some of the difficult, skill demanding actions in lessons on Flight, or On- and Off-balance.

Clever body management is also needed for lowering and raising the body while walking, running or travelling in other ways. The weight can be lowered through kneeling, sitting or lying, and be raised again with fluency and without stopping. All superfluous movements should be eliminated and generally the hands should not touch the floor, although ways should be discovered of using the arms to assist by giving direction or impetus to the action. Such practices develop nimbleness in getting down to the floor and off it with ease. Spinning, twisting and turning movements while sinking or rising or both, can aid in the adjustments of the weight, and the curving, swirling movements help to give continuity in action. Continuity is often broken by the checking effect of new parts of the body touching the ground to take the weight, and stopping can be avoided by anticipating how to keep the trunk moving. The leg action must also be anticipated for the legs must get ready to receive and lift the weight. Many people can be helped to feel how to make a logical sequence of events by taking a few practice turns of the lowering, weight changes and rising in slow motion.

Weight bearing on hands and feet and 'wheeling' actions

Actions in which weight is transferred to the hands and back to the feet, form the basis of many skills. Children invent ways of walking, running and jumping using both hands and feet. They should be encouraged to try out the many possible combinations, e g both feet and both hands, two feet and one hand, one of each and so on, and learn to move fluently in all directions and at all speeds. They should also experience placing the hands in various relations to the body, not only in front, and to lift, kick or swing the legs round the hands, to land in various places, away from the place of take-off, and to be resilient and agile enough to make several consecutive movements, hopping and scuttling about all over the floor. The activities demand flexibility and many adjustments of weight, and they increase the manoeuverability of the body. The ability to twist and move the body while the weight is borne by the hands makes possible the weight adjustments which will prevent heedless falls while handstanding, if balance is lost.

Tasks of balancing or transferring weight over the hands are much practised gymnastic skills and greatly enjoyed by many children. Handstanding can be approached in an exploratory way as described above, to give confidence in being on the hands and upside down, as well as to give experience of how to adjust the weight to prevent harmful falling. Tasks in which the weight passes over the hands, cartwheel-like, are safer than handstanding on a symmetrical base where there is danger of over-swinging and falling on the back. The cartwheel-like actions can be done with many different leg movements, legs together, one following the other, bent legs or stretched legs, and they are more fun and skilful if several consecutive 'wheels' are made, first in one direction, then back again the other way. As skill improves the movement can be widened, extended and slowed down.

Ways of travelling and balancing with one leg stretched high and the other held low helps youngsters to feel their balance in handstanding. Handstanding against a wall or to a partner is unhelpful in the long run. It is most important to learn how to adjust one's weight and be self-reliant from the beginning. There is, however, the exception who will benefit from being supported by the teacher who knows how to help in order to develop independence. When people are confident on their arms, sure of their balance and know how to save themselves, they experiment further by balancing in various shapes (curled up close to the hands or stretched out, long or wide, far from them), by moving their legs while balancing, by removing one hand to balance on the other, by marking time, walking, running and even jumping on the hands.

Youngsters can also be set to discover several ways of wheeling which can be done around the various axes of the body. Cartwheeling is done round a sagittal axis, handstanding and over is round a side to side horizontal axis, and by starting on all fours, facing or back to the ground (crab position) it is possible to progress sideways by turning over and over, round the vertical axis running from head to tail, through the spine. The two latter actions are very strenuous and they also require great mobility and resilience, therefore practices should be short to avoid any possibility of strain.

Tasks concerned with ways of coming down from handstanding should be given because these should also be controlled and resilient. The commonest way of landing is on to one leg which should prepare to receive the weight, then yield resiliently as the weight comes on to it, and react with elasticity, as in all landings. The yielding should continue until the whole weight is over the receiving foot and then the resilient recovery to uprightness is made. Many people do not allow the receiving leg to yield as the weight is received and this results in an ungainly movement in which the trunk is levered from the hip, on a stiff leg, into the upright position. By yielding more fully the whole body takes a share in both lowering and lifting the body. If balance is lost the yielding should continue to the floor, and the movement go on in rolling, before recovery. Less yielding in the receiving leg is needed in wheeling actions in which momentum carries the weight onward over the leg, and the lifting phase of the recovery starts while the weight is passing over the receiving leg.

Some youngsters inevitably try to lower the weight from handstanding on to the shoulders or chest, to roll over the back or rock on the front. A few even direct their weight to land and rock on one side but all these actions can cause strains and jarring unless they are carefully controlled. Those who yield too quickly and hold themselves too slackly are liable to jar their backs or necks. In moving from a handstand into a forward roll it is essential when the body is lowered to see that the head is tucked forward so that the back of the neck and shoulders, rounded areas, touch first. Most people have to learn to resist the speed of the fall by keeping a firm grip of the body and by holding the legs high over the supporting regions, to counteract the downward pull. If the legs crumple as soon as the fall starts, the downward movement of the hips is too fast and the tendency is to drop on to a flattened back. It is a challenge to make the action slow and smooth until the weight is safely on the rounded upper back, after which the recovery can start at much greater speed. Similarly, in lowering on to the front or one side, a strong upward extension resists the speed of fall as well as preparing a fully extended 'rocker' to receive the weight. This type of skill should never be presented as a task which the whole class is expected to pursue.

Apparatus work

Every type of apparatus work, climbing, swinging, hanging, jumping, tumbling, rolling and balancing can be used in lessons on Transference of Weight. A selection of apparatus work should be made which gives experience of all these activities, and they should be chosen to develop further the ideas explored and practised in Part I of the lesson, the floorwork. The activities mentioned above can very often be combined in sequences of actions and this makes it easier to ensure that all types are represented.

Suggestions for typical ways of:

Hanging, climbing and swinging

Moving along bars or poles of various height, hanging under or supported on top.

Climbing up, down, across or all combined on window ladders or wall bars.

Jumping up to hang or swing on ropes, and coming down to make the first 'touch down' with various parts of the body.

Swinging to lift the weight on to forms, bars or boxes.

Jumping

Jumping to 'arrive' on to forms, boxes and other vaulting apparatus, to hold balance on various parts of the body, followed by transferring the weight off the apparatus by springing, wheeling, sliding or rolling.

Crossing apparatus with the weight on the arms or various other parts.

Leaping or 'stepping' from one piece of apparatus to another, and from higher to lower apparatus and vice versa.

Leaping to get on to the apparatus to roll or rock, on or along it.

Tumbling and rolling

Rolling or other ways of transferring weight along the length of an agility mattress (this can be made more exciting and difficult by putting the mattress across two or more forms or rolling up mats to make humps on the course).

Rolling, sliding or tumbling down or up an incline. (The incline can be made by storming boards or several forms close together, inclined on wall bars, bars or window ladders. Care is needed in rolling down because of the momentum gathered.)

Rolling and springing up alternately, along a series of mats arranged in line, or two mats at right angles, or three mats in a wide triangle.

Rolling along or over forms or boxes, and rolling off apparatus, via hands from apparatus of any height, or tumbling off without help of hands from low heights. (Care is needed to avoid jarring.)

Balancing and sliding

Sliding down sloping forms while balancing on various parts.

Spinning on a body part while crossing apparatus.

Jumping or swinging to 'arrive' on apparatus.

Crawling and transferring weight in other ways along narrow apparatus.

Outline of progression

Themes based on Transference of Weight are, on the whole, elementary and most suitable for beginners. Ingenious, adventurous first year beginners enjoy everything including all forms of rocking and rolling, but older, more sophisticated beginners would be unlikely to enjoy rolling on the floor, but might be interested in learning to master their balance, in finding various ways of receiving their weight and discovering how to manage themselves in various 'step-like' actions.

This work is preparatory for Flight and Actions emphasising Balance. Work drawn from this source is often used in Part I of lessons, but lessons based entirely on Transference of Weight would, on the whole, be inappropriate for more advanced classes.

TRAVELLING

Travelling, like Weight Transference, is a form of locomotion but the difference lies in the purpose for moving. Travelling describes actions in which the intention is to move through space from place to place, whereas Weight Transference has a bodily stress of moving from part to part of the body, and the movement through space is only incidental. The actions are superficially similar but if the performer's intention is clear, the difference can be felt and it is also observable. Travelling includes a great variety of actions and gives opportunity for the use of ingenuity and the development of versatility. Through these actions youngsters learn to share the general space and to move nimbly and safely without collisions and with awareness of others, all important safety factors.

In planning themes based on the concept of Travelling, the teacher selects material and gives guidance on many scores which will help to give experience and understanding of everything that is involved in the idea of Travelling.

One can travel on many *different parts of the body*, and the whole evolution of locomotion can be re-experienced, travelling reptile-like on the body, with or without the help of the limbs (soldiers and stalkers progress so), crawling (needed for recovering control in off-balance jumps or when falling), walking and other modes of progression on the feet, and moving on bent legs (as Russian dancers), or with straight legs and with various leg gestures. One can travel by rolling, 'walking' on the shins, seat or alternate sides of the body, and by walking on the hands or even running or jumping on them, and many forms of hopping and jumping also involve travelling (page 40).

Variations of speed should be made and there should be moments of travelling very fast contrasted with moving much more slowly. The youngsters should be encouraged to become so nimble that they can travel at great speed on their feet and other parts of the body, in and out of people and things. At a later stage it is a test of control to increase and decrease the speed of movement gradually. This experience can be exploited in actions such as accelerating for a jump and decelerating after landing. The rhythm of working up and dying down is needed in gymnastics generally, and particularly for control in vaulting and jumping. Many actions can also be done slowly and it demands concentration to keep control of every part of a 'step' (page 26). Big, resilient steps moving on the feet, or slow wheeling movements over the hands are generally interesting to people who are beyond the beginner stage, a stage when they show great desire to become skilful and improve the quality and form of their work. Not all actions can sensibly be done either quickly or slowly, many have a natural speed and rhythm, e g rocking, swinging or leaping, so one must teach people to discriminate, but whenever the body is supported it is possible to control and vary the speed. The speed of many locomotor actions can, therefore, be changed and gravity need only dictate the speed when the body is unsupported in the air.

Moving and stopping should also be contrasted. Beginners enjoy getting up speed and stopping suddenly and more experienced people can do the same but with more control and precision, and they can also experience the contrast of moving fluently through every part of the room with the sensation of broken movement produced by spurts of dashing and stopping, moving as one often does in games, alternately hovering on the spot and shooting off to a new place. A short burst of movement with instant stopping, sometimes with a sharp turn, or a sudden pounce down to the ground, can be exciting to do and gives experience of checking and holding the body motionless, and so increases control (page 101).

The spatial aspects are stressed through the use of all directions, forward, backward, sideways or round, and by using various pathways by travelling zigzag, in a twisty way or straight, and by moving through, and on, various levels. By means of Travelling actions youngsters can become aware of how to use the general space. They learn to use it well by becoming conscious of the space around them and things in it, and are then able to dash, dodge, check and stop without collisions. To make this more demanding, the available space can be reduced so that people learn to be nimble while moving in a restricted area, and this should be contrasted with the freedom which is felt when the space is opened up again (page 127).

After the beginner stage people should be taught to *phrase* their movement. In common with all actions, modes of Travelling should have a beginning, a middle part of the movement and an end, and unless this happens, the travelling often becomes aimless and vague. A starting position which gives readiness to go should be chosen. If a sudden, energetic dash to a new place is coming, the starting position must be firm, with readiness to thrust the weight away. If light and fluent movement is anticipated the starting position should be one in which the body is lightly poised, ready to move. Travelling should also be made purposeful by going from one place to another pre-determined place, or by moving about with the intention of seeking gaps to dash through, or by making a winding journey in the available space. There must also be a definite ending. Sometimes movement dies down gradually to a gentle stop, but the ending can also be abrupt, and then the body is gripped and held firmly, in order to arrest all movement. There should be no inconclusive fading out at the end of a phrase and the final position should often be a reflection of the quality of movement which preceded it.

Ordinary good *walking* should be taught, and should be practised, if appropriate, in most gymnastics lessons. People do not, on the whole, naturally walk well in the present day, therefore, through their movement education they should learn to walk with more poise and grace. Walking, like carriage of the body, is much influenced by personality and current moods and trends, and if the teacher observes that the youngsters respond in a self-conscious or disinterested way, walking as an exercise, should be avoided until it proves more propitious to introduce it. To give more awareness of what is involved in walking, one would deal with the use of the foot in stepping, the poise of the body, the arm and leg swing and the rhythm. To increase awareness of different parts of the foot, all parts of it can be tested for weight taking, the ball and toes, the toes only, the heels, the outer and inner border (the latter very briefly and only for the sake of the experience), and this should lead to stepping with rocking over the heel and along the outer border of the foot to the ball and toes, while the weight is transferred over the leading leg. This must become automatic as soon as possible so that the action of walking can be felt as a whole, with an even length of step on to resilient legs, a well poised body with head held high, and an easy arm swing from the shoulder to oppose and balance the leg swing. The arm swing equals the leg swing; with small steps the arms make a small swing, with longer steps, the arm swing also increases. The aim should be to develop a natural rhythmic, fluent way of walking. Artificial ways, stepping with the toes first, may have a place in drama or dance, or for the sake of the experience in gymnastics to contrast it with natural walking, but such contrived ways have no real part in gymnastics. Walking backward and progressing sideways, with easy changes of direction, are appropriate as they are often necessary and useful for games as well as for the movement of everyday life. Natural walking can be difficult in the environment of the gymnasium but it becomes less so if it is done purposefully by moving from one pre-determined place to another.

Apparatus work

Typical Travelling actions which include apparatus are:

Rolling along mattresses, form or boxes.

Balancing along narrow surfaces, or moving up and down from one height to another and negotiating obstacles by going over, under or through them.

Sliding down or along apparatus.

Climbing on wall bars, window ladders, and all types of ropes.

Travelling suspended under or supported on apparatus.

Leaping using apparatus as obstacles in the course.

In order to carry out the idea of Travelling, a journey must be made which has a starting point and a finishing place, and this can be done by arranging apparatus in a track to be followed or a circuit to be made. Tracks can be as simple as going along the length of a form, or much more complex, like a commando course, e.g. using a rope to swing to a box, to reach a rope ladder supporting an inclined form on which to get down. Circuits are round journeys; an elementary circuit might include mats, forms, wall bars or window ladders arranged so that all pieces are used in making a round trip.

Tracks and circuits can both include:

Use of slopes made by inclining forms or planks on to anything which will safely hold them. They can be made mobile by attaching them to ropes, rings or trapeze (care is needed to see that they are safely attached). The slopes can vary in inclination and also in width, and two or three forms close together on a bar or wall bar, make a sloping platform. Slopes can be used for all forms of travelling including rolling, and can be made more comfortable by putting a mattress over the slope.

Climbing and suspension travelling making use of all types of fixed apparatus for a journey keeping off the floor, e g across a series of ropes or round and along a series of poles.

Use of obstacles placed in various formations for hurdling over, or for getting under, over, round, along or on and off, e g three forms in zigzag formation for travelling along, or several Danish balancing bars placed crosswise for getting over or on and off to traverse over all the bars.

Clearing gaps. The track or circuit may include a gap which has to be cleared, e.g. from wall bars to a mat, or by swinging on a rope to reach a form, bar or box, or by springing from one piece of apparatus to another, with a gap between. The gap to be cleared can be on the same level, or from low to high, or the reverse.

Balancing can form part of a track or circuit.

Any of these suggestions can be used in a simple form, the whole journey might consist of rolling down or up a long slope, or of getting along a bar from upright to upright, but many combinations of apparatus and actions can be arranged to make exciting journeys. Some people have difficulty in linking a series of actions in an easy and simple way, and it may help them to look first at everything in the track, all the surfaces, levels, slopes, angles and spaces formed by the apparatus and the floor, and then with greater awareness of the situation, be able to anticipate as they go. To be satisfying, one action must lead logically to the next and tracks and circuits should, therefore, be experienced as a whole rather than as a series of disconnected parts.

Outline of progression

Lessons based on the idea of Travelling are suitable at every stage. First year beginners are interested in exploring the whole range of actions in a free and lively way, without too much stress on precision, but with particular emphasis on using all parts of the body, the general space, changes of direction, changes of speed, and going and stopping. After this stage children become interested in developing their skill and, therefore, more attention should be given to precision of bodily action and quality of movement in such skills as the wheeling actions and in sequences of receiving the weight, as described on pages 26 and 28. At an intermediate stage they should also learn how to phrase movement and pay attention to starting positions and ways of ending as well as the main parts of the action. Ordinary, graceful, resilient walking might, at a certain stage, particularly interest adolescent girls, and if so, the opportunity should be seized to teach them how to walk well.

Travelling actions, which at the same time test skill in balancing, are suitable for both the intermediate and advanced stages. To control balance is always an absorbing task, and this can be planned so that it ranges from simple to very advanced, according to the skill of the group. Several sections in the apparatus work can be given a balancing bias by including actions such as stepping or jumping across gaps, or by balancing along narrow apparatus while at the same time surmounting and negotiating obstacles. Leaping or swinging to arrive on a narrow surface is also absorbing, and the difficulty can be increased by making the gaps bigger and by making the apparatus higher.

Many actions can include Partner or Group work in which people help one another up on to, down from and along apparatus, and they can change places and interweave without coming off the apparatus. Some of these actions need very precise movement, accurate gestures and placing of weight bearing parts, and controlled weight transference, and this is the type of work which should be practised in Part I of the lesson.

Action Themes

Weight bearing and weight transference.
Travelling.
Control of body weight.
Receiving the weight.
Moving and stopping.
Locomotion.

Each of these themes has a particular emphasis which must be brought out through lessons on the subject.

FLIGHT

Flight is the term used to describe the specialised form of locomotion in which one leaves the ground and flies through the air. This happens in jumping and leaping as well as in actions such as cat springs, dives on to the hands, and all forms of hopping and springing, and these are true flights. The term Assisted Flight is given to actions in which springing and flying are emphasised but partners or apparatus are used to support the body during the flight. To leap, jump and fly is the most exciting part of gymnastics, and the exhilaration it gives is highly satisfying. The exhilaration comes from a sense of mastery, a defiance of gravity, a power over one's weight and a sense of freedom, and the excitement stems from the daring which is needed and from taking an adventurous risk.

There are three clearly distinguishable parts in the actions of leaping, jumping and flying:

The take-off which is concerned with how to get off the ground to fly into the air.

The flight which is the phase in the air.

The landing which concerns coming to earth with skill.

These parts are all closely related and interdependent.

The take-off

The take-off is the part of the action which projects the body into the air. It is most usual to spring from one or both legs but it is possible to take off from other parts of the body such as the shins, hips or arms.

Spring is developed through repetitive hops (springing on one leg) and jumps (springing from two legs) since these bouncy movements increase elasticity and strength of leg. The intricate springing apparatus formed by the toes, feet, ankles, knees and hips must all work actively and with perfect co-ordination to gain full effect from the springing. All joints extend explosively and fully to shoot the body up and to use the elasticity and resilience of the legs effectively. It is important that the take-off should be a continuous movement, the downward pressure leading without pause straight into the upward thrust, the change over being the moment of greatest speed and power. Many children make the mistake of crouching down too low and then stopping at the lowest point, and this annuls any recoiling powers of the muscles which play so great a part in generating spring.

Not only must the leg action be co-ordinated but the way the rest of the body is held and controlled influences the result. For hopping and jumping the body must be held in a light grip with vitality and good balance. Many people hold themselves too slackly so that in every jump the impact with the ground makes them flop like a rag doll, and this upsets their balance, throws them about and breaks the pulsing rhythm. If before starting to jump, they are helped to get a grip of themselves by taking a light tension in their arms, chest, waist, hips and legs, and to lift away from the floor, they will feel more animation in their bodies and this will give them more control. Much practice of hopping and jumping is needed to develop full range of movement in the feet and legs. It is necessary because of the incomplete and insensitive way the feet and legs are used and the body carried in daily life. Muscular slackness, inco-ordination and bad habits all have to be counteracted if springing is to be buoyant and well co-ordinated.

It is easier to bounce on the spot than to do so while travelling but as skill increases both should be mastered. Tasks can be given of making sequences based on hops or jumps on the spot alternating with springing while travelling. The interludes on the spot allow control and balance to be regained. Even greater skill and control are needed for travelling with a series of big springs (hopping, jumping, skipping, galloping, also with turning and changes of direction). Similarly, fast travelling with tiny jumps requires very good foot-work, good control of the body and general nimbleness and agility. Such actions should be broken up into short phrases and made rhythmical by alternating movement with short, active pauses.

More experienced people can get the necessary practice in hopping and jumping by composing sequences of single or double starts combined with landing on one or both feet. These sequences can be worked out to give every possible combination of take-off and landing. They are also interesting as simple apparatus work when using forms, springboards or beating boards. In all jumps the ability to adjust bodily tension and remain poised is essential for success, but in the long run this all depends on liveliness of mind which brings vitality to the body.

Single and double start

The flight depends on the effectiveness of the take-off which can be from two feet, double start, or one foot, single start. A single start arises quite naturally from running, the last step being a strong spring, powerful enough to shoot the body into the air. To make a double start, the legs are gathered after the last running step and a powerful upward jump is made from both legs together.

In any take-off the whole body acts as a spring which is first compressed and then suddenly released in a vigorous extension away from the point of support, in the direction of the jump. The power comes from the explosive extension of the hips, knees, ankles, feet and toes thrusting against a resistant surface. No lifting power is wasted if the thrust is transmitted through the centre of gravity and up through the body. If the body is extended and the chest and sternum lifted, the body position will be such that the power can be transmitted through it. The timing of the stretching and the degree of tension must be accurately judged to prevent jerking or over arching and thereby upsetting balance and spoiling the spring. An effective take-off must be well timed, and for jumps off boards or for vaulting it must also be in the right place (page 48f). Few children have any problem with a single start as it is a natural action, but some need help in co-ordinating a double start as they find difficulty in timing the gathering of the legs and then, without pause, springing up. Simple actions such as one step followed by several double jumps give the feeling of how to gather the legs and jump up. Several jumps are needed at first; if only one jump is made, there is a tendency to land, rather than spring up. A few approach steps should be added when the first practice is mastered. To develop accuracy in both types of start, it is often a help to make a target to bounce away from, such as a circle on the ground or a mark on the top of a form. The target is used as a place to bounce from to send the child up and away. The timing and upward stress of the take-off can be further emphasised by shooting up one arm or other part of the body. These suggestions are only given as an indication of the type of thing which might help to overcome these technical difficulties, but it is essential for the teacher to study each child's own problems and give help accordingly.

Jumping from various parts of the body

Children can experiment with bouncing from various parts of the body, this type of jump is often used for getting off apparatus, e g from seat or shins. Many enjoy a game of jumping from one part of the body to another, such as from one hip, to shins, to feet, and they will practise until they can do it with ease, resilience and continuity. Bouncing on these unusual parts of the body depends on ability to gather and release power explosively to throw the body into the air; all parts help by pressing down towards the weight bearing parts and then, without pause, thrusting away from the floor. All parts assist by rising and making the adjustments which will allow the power of the thrust to be transmitted through the body. If people can feel this and relate the experience to all jumping, they become more aware of the sensation of gathering and releasing power, and in this way may improve their spring.

Jumping from feet to hands and hands to feet produces a variety of skills including catsprings and all forms of handsprings. They can be high or long springs, and can also be done with twists and changes of direction. Agility and resilience are developed through such springs, and as skill increases several successive springs should be demanded to develop nimbleness and give greater fluency of movement.

The airborne phase of the flight

The flight starts as soon as the body is airborne and lasts until some part touches down. Flights can be in various directions, such as diving forward into space, springing off to one side, but generally elevation is emphasised. Some people appear to rocket up like a projectile, holding considerable tension while they soar through the air, while others, having become airborne, release much of the tension and hold themselves lightly, sailing in the air, seeming to be suspended. Some prefer the strong leaps and some the lighter ones, but those who are really versatile will enjoy both.

Experiments to stress specific parts of the body in jumping and leaping gives valuable experience in mastering the body. Lifting the sternum increases the sensation of elevation, but equally well other parts, such as one side of the chest or one shoulder, can give the same feeling. The lower parts of the body can be emphasised in the same way, one or both knees can be flung up and the hips can 'punch' into the air, carrying the body with them. The legs can swing in various directions, one after the other or to join in the air, and the feet can be whipped to various places in relation to the body, close underneath or to one side. The tendency is for the body to sink if the legs are lifted and this must be counteracted by a conscious effort to make the whole body rise, with all the parts helping it to do so. Specific parts of the body are also stressed in turning jumps. The head, shoulders, arms, hips, one knee or leg can all initiate a twist which will take the body into a turning jump. This selection of parts of the body for a specific role is a potent way of increasing awareness in isolated parts, and this is a requirement for complete mastery. But though one part is stressed, always every other part is in action, adjustments are needed in the whole body to give form and to keep balance and poise.

The whole body is stressed in various movements which can be made during the flight. It is possible to:

> Bend in all directions, arching backwards, curving sideways, or rounding forward.
> Elongate the body in various directions in space.
> Spread out away from or draw in towards the centre of the body.
> Twist or turn, or both.
> Make various body shapes.
> Move symmetrically or asymmetrically.
> Move the body throughout the flight.

Double or single starts can project the body into space. Double starts lead more naturally to symmetrical jumps, but it is also possible to move asymmetrically after the take-off, as in twisting or arching to one side. A powerful single take-off leads to great bounds or leaps with a one-sided stress, in which it is possible to assume a variety of asymmetrical shapes. Exploration of different body shapes which arise from single or double starts, and experiments to discover the effects of moving specific parts of the body while jumping, is the type of work which is suitable for those beyond the beginner stage who are fast becoming skilful. The intricate leaps which can be invented will stretch even the highly skilled.

There should be a definite *climax* in such flights, a part of the flight which is particularly emphasised in which every part of the action reaches its peak, everything culminating in a clear body shape. Split-second timing is needed to achieve this. Sometimes the shape is held for an appreciable time before it is released in preparation for the landing. Skilled people can delay the moment of release, and in spite of descending, hold their flight position until the very last moment. One sees Ballet dancers doing this, and it is shown in slow motion when a male dancer slowly lowers his partner, who holds her position until, and even after, she touches the floor. Much exciting partner work in gymnastics can be done in this way, one catching and holding the other in various positions, before lowering and releasing one another.

Many people when jumping are so concerned about their arrival that they hurry the whole flight, achieve no climax and feel no elevation or moment of suspension. Many release the grip of their bodies too soon and so become heavy and slack in the air, which makes the landing all the more difficult to manage. The most interesting and exciting jumps are those which have a prolonged period of flight as when jumping off apparatus or from swinging ropes, but very high free jumps can be made by getting impetus for the spring by means of an accelerated run leading up to the take-off. The spring can be greatly augmented by the use of springboards or trampettes.

Landings and recoveries

Adroit management of the body on landing is a safety measure and it is essential that people should know how to cope with themselves when they land. Skilful control prevents jarring of body, straining and wrenching of joints, bruising and other injuries. The main qualities needed for good and effective landings are elasticity, resilience and strength of leg and a feeling for how the body is poised and balanced. Many gymnastic activities contribute to developing these. The hopping and jumping described in Take-off increase suppleness and resilience of feet and legs. Resilient bouncing in a bent knee position (knee springs) can develop feeling for the momentary release of tension in the legs which occurs in the change over from the dropping to the lifting phase of the movement. The elasticity of the powerful leg muscles should be exploited, and if it is used effectively, much unnecessary hard work is eliminated. A resilient rebound is the main factor which makes deep landings so easy and effortless and youngsters should be taught the knack of 'catching the bounce'. Strength and resilience of legs are further developed if a strong upward spring is made between each bounce. This should be a powerful extension of the legs and body to shoot the body high into the air before it drops lightly down again in the next landing. Several successive springs, catching the bounce each time, produce the feeling of elasticity and resilience which gives the needed quality of movement. The activities can be presented as tasks and be done in an inventive way on the spot or with locomotion, with changes of direction and with twisting and turning in the air, but the exercises are very strenuous and should not be overdone. Short spells, often repeated, are much more effective than one or two long and tiring turns. Many of the activities described in Transference of Weight also contribute to skill in landing and recovering.

Principles of Landing

Most landings are made on to one or both feet but it is possible to land on the hands or other parts of the body. The way of landing depends on the flight and the balance of the body, when it touches down. The speed and the part of the body receiving the weight also make a difference to the way the landing and recovery are made. People become safe and competent through constant practice and by experimenting with ways of coming down and transferring weight, and as they learn to understand the principles, they become able to adapt and discover how to cope with themselves however they land.

The important points to impress when teaching landings are:

To prepare for the landing.

To yield resiliently to absorb the shock of impact.

To move nimbly immediately after landing to reduce the pressure on weight bearing parts.

To feel the direction of movement and go with it until control is gained, except when movement is deliberately arrested or direction purposely changed. This is in order to reduce the danger of straining or wrenching any part of the body.

These principles should emerge while landings are being taught and practised.

Buoyant and yielding landings

The two fundamentally different ways of landing depend mainly on how the body is balanced and the on force of coming down. Yielding softly, right down to the ground should occur if the body is unbalanced or coming down from a great height, but when the body is well balanced the feeling of the lift and buoyancy of the flight can be maintained while landing lightly and resiliently. In both cases, one prepares by keeping a grip of the body and by reaching out towards the place of landing, ready to adjust on touching down by yielding to the falling weight, without at this moment, checking the speed of fall. (A check causes jarring and makes the landing harsh, painful and noisy). Yielding in the feet, ankles and knees should occur instantly in all landings. (The hips yield but this is incidental and need not be stressed). In the yielding type of landing, the whole body yields, together with the legs, so that the relaxed body drops softly to the ground, but in time to avert a complete collapse the weight is caught and the body is redirected into a roll or other form of weight transference, and the recovery follows this movement. The other type of landing has a more buoyant feeling and even when the body is falling there is no general sensation of yielding, instead one holds on to the feeling of being up, airborne, and light, and when the toes touch, only the feet and legs yield, instantly and resiliently, and the elastic recoiling movement immediately bounces the body up again. The landings with total yielding are, generally speaking, more elementary than the buoyant type. Beginners and young children are safer if their whole attention is concentrated on yielding and letting go. Greater skill, strength, resilience, sense of balance, timing and feeling for movement are needed for the buoyant type of landing.

Various ways of landing and recovering

Landing on both legs together can be done in vaults and jumps in which the body is balanced and vertical. The legs are held together for firmness and strength and the better protection of the feet and knees. The body drops and lands lightly if, instantly on touching down, the legs yield through full flexion of the knees. The reaction of the elastic legs is to spring back in a resilient recoiling movement which, with only a slight additional effort, will shoot the body up again. An upright poise with the hips vertically over the feet is needed for these light, elastic landings. It is not always necessary to go through a full flexion of the knees, but landings which are checked in semiflexion are often very taut, jerky and hard because sheer strength is used, rather than elasticity and resilience. When balance is disturbed in the flight or by the landing, the reaction should be to yield right down and toss the body into a roll to recover in a springy way, or more calmly, once the feet touch the ground again.

Landing on one leg should never be done from any appreciable height since there is always time to gather the legs and land more safely on both. Landing on one leg is a much smaller, quicker movement in which the yielding and recovery consists of a rocking movement in the foot from toe to heel and back again, to coincide with the yielding and springing phases of the leg. The receiving leg is prepared with a slight outward turn which makes allowance for any lateral deviation in balance, and the knee will fall more readily over the foot as the leg yields, if the whole leg is rotated outwards, and in this way strained knees and feet can be avoided. When leaping higher and travelling faster the receiving foot touches lightly and only momentarily, and the yielding is followed immediately by a quick recoiling movement and a swift change of weight on to the other foot, and the recovery is a running movement during which the weight is brought into full control.

Landing while turning poses further problems because when landing on one leg the receiving foot and ankle are in special danger as the foot is stopped by touching the ground while the body continues to revolve. Therefore, the receiving foot should be released as soon as possible in quick, light changes of weight from foot to foot. If the landing is on to both feet, small jumps to change the position of the feet is a way of gaining control, and in both landings the speed is reduced gradually while the body rotates. These landings can be made in a buoyant way if the body is balanced but if it is unbalanced before the arrival or by the landing, the yielding should occur while the whole body sinks and continues to spin, and the recovery is made by travelling and turning on the hands and feet or on other parts of the body until the momentum dies down and control is restored.

Landing on the hands should also be mastered. To do this the hands and arms act in the same way as the legs. The fingers reach out to the place of arrival, preparing to receive the weight which is taken successively on fingers, hands and heel of hands, with the wrists, elbows and shoulders yielding with resistance to prevent a collapse on to the floor. In big, vigorous jumps such as catsprings, the arms reach out and the landing resists the forward impetus but with an elastic yielding followed instantly by a pushing back to thrust the upper part of the body up and back over the feet. In some of the high vertical dives on to the hands, the arms check the speed with which the body comes to the ground before rolling. Diving and rolling need good co-ordination, ability to control tension, skill in fast rolling, and should only be permitted if the teacher is satisfied that the children have the skill to cope.

Landing on the body is sometimes unavoidable when falling and when this happens a resilient limb should, if possible, reach out to check the speed and take the first shock of the impact but the limb must on no account be stiff or resist the fall. The body should be rounded so that the weight can be transferred quickly away from the part which first touched and it should be kept travelling in the direction of motion. If the body is kept moving the first touch can be light and momentary, and it is generally possible to adjust so that this can happen and so that angular parts such as the point of the elbow or knee do not receive the brunt of the weight. Flat falls on to large areas of the body may cause shock, winding and bruising, and they can be dangerous. Difficulties can generally be avoided by the rapid movement over rounded surfaces and by twisting a convenient part of the body into the path of the movement. To give experience in a safe way, these landings should be practised close to the floor at first, from low starting positions such as kneeling, sitting or lying on a form, then tumbling off and rolling away.

Landing and stopping instantly may be necessary sometimes through lack of space or the need to change direction. Children often drop from a height on to all fours like a cat, and they should practise this and become adept in it for they can land safely and with stability in this way in a small space. All the limbs should react with elastic, springy movement. Leaps and jumps can also be arrested instantly when landing on the feet by gripping the ground firmly and letting the strong legs make only a slight give. It is easiest to land with the feet apart, knees springy, and the feet touching down simultaneously or one immediately after the other. The direction of motion must be counteracted partly by resistance from the legs and partly by the way the feet are placed with a wide base, in line with the motion, and with one foot in advance of the centre of gravity. A resistance in the body, against the direction of motion, also checks the body, for example, a turning movement is checked by a counter twist in the body before or at the moment of landing.

Apparatus work
Use of boards and trampettes

Beating boards, springboards and trampettes are specially designed to give added impetus to flight, but when they are introduced children should be at a stage where they are skilful enough to judge their run exactly so that the take-off comes once only on the most resilient part of the apparatus. A beating board does little more than give a raised start, but a springboard has elasticity and, if used correctly, can impart considerable impetus to the body. Trampettes are even more elastic and consequently have a much greater effect.

On first using a springboard children should be encouraged to test its potential. By jumping about all over it they can discover exactly which is the most springy part of the board and then work out how to co-ordinate a run with a take-off from the springiest part. Single and double starts should be mastered; some children find one easier than the other. Those who have no difficulty can immediately progress to all types of exciting flights. Others may need help to get the timing and rhythm right, as well as finding the best place to bounce on the board. While this is a problem they generally find it interesting and absorbing, and it is time well spent because it is a skill which should be practised until it becomes 'automatic', so that in jumping and vaulting the whole attention can be given to the flight. The pressure of the weight makes the board recoil and this sends the body up. The more rigid the board, the quicker and smaller is the recoiling movement and, therefore, the speed of the take-off must be adjusted to the springiness of the board. Stress must be placed on coming off the board, up into the air, and the body must be firm and balanced in order to benefit from the impetus imparted to it.

Progressive steps in the use of the trampette

A trampette is very elastic and should be used with caution. Unless people can manage their bodies, are able to hold a grip of themselves in the air, have had experience in a great variety of leaps and jumps and landings, there is no point in using a trampette for springing. Through lack of confidence and understanding they will be unable to use it efficiently and will build up bad habits, and if they do happen to use it with any force, they are liable either to be thrown into a forward rotation and fall head first or be thrown backward to fall on their backs, which is both dangerous and frightening. When youngsters have enough command of themselves to be fit to use a trampette, there are progressive steps which will lead to an understanding of the effect of the trampette and give confidence in the use of it. People can first be set to discover the effect of bouncing on the trampette on various parts of the body such as knees or hips, before trying small jumps on the feet. Obviously they know theoretically what will happen but it is quite a different matter to experience in reality what effect their weight has on the trampette and subsequently on themselves. The next step is to feel body balance while bouncing on the feet, and this should be done either with the help of two climbing ropes to hold with the trampette between, or with the help of a partner standing in front, or a partner on each side, lightly holding the performer's hands to assist balance.

Use is made of the ropes or partners according to skill, some may cling tightly while others barely touch them. Partners have the duty of helping sensitively, according to need, and also watching that the performer stays in the centre of the platform. The next progresssion is to jump from the trampette on to a single rope. The rope should hang about a yard from the front edge of the trampette. At first a gentle run up to the trampette is made, followed without pause, by a drop on to the platform and a take-off to spring forward and up on to the rope. This can be practised until it can be done with ease and confidence. This step leads to free flights, and when these are first tried it is important to stress that the direction must be forward and up as if one were jumping up on to the rope. The arms, head and upper part of the body must be lifted in order to give balance. A double start, which throws the weight symmetrically, should be used before jumps from single starts are tried, since these throw the body asymmetrically.

When simple actions have been mastered more daring flights can be tried and then the trampette can be approached from various angles. It is enjoyable to jump down from a height on to a springboard or trampette for one is bounced up and 'thrown away' in an exciting manner. Combining a trampette with vaulting apparatus, as an aid to vaulting, is advanced gymnastics and careful consideration should be given to the matter before making such arrangements. The point of a trampette is to throw the body high, and this should give a flight before touching the apparatus, with a considerable time lag between the take-off and the touch down (or, the flight may be right over the apparatus without touching at all), and this demands both courage and skill, for great accuracy and judgment are needed to keep control of the body, not to miss the apparatus and to cope with the landing from such a height.

The placing and use of springboards are also a matter for thought. They, too, throw the body up so that the effect of the spring should be considered in relation to the height and position of the apparatus and how it is to be used. When the body is to be inverted and supported on the arms, upside down, the apparatus can be relatively low, for the hips have to be lifted so high. On the other hand, upright vaults need higher apparatus, high enough for the arms to have to make a lifting and pushing movement, while the hips, kept low, pass between or round the arms. For flying vaults over the length of the apparatus, the board must be placed far enough back to allow the vaulter to spring up and forward from the springy part of the board without catching on the near edge of the apparatus.

Vaulting and agility in flight

Every type of apparatus can be used for Flight. In true flights it is used for leaping on to, off, over or round, and a push or pull may be made on the apparatus to augment the flight. Assisted Flights need the help of partners to support the weight during the flight, and partners can help each other to fly on to or over the apparatus or down from it. Ropes, rings or trapezes can carry the weight in flying swings, and poles can be grasped while the performer flies whizzing around them.

From a very young age children enjoy jumping off things, 'flying down'. They scramble up on to things and jump off, grading the height according to their courage. In gymnastics, when children are left free to experiment this is often what they do by choice especially if the apparatus is too high to jump on to or over easily. Through this experience they first gain skill in landing and later become more adventurous with the flight. Children also elect to jump over all the obstacles in their path, sometimes without touching and sometimes leaning or pushing with a foot, lower leg, hip, one or both arms. These natural activities of children later emerge, in more developed form, as gymnastics skills. They develop into:

High and long jumps such as the free jumps already described and jumps making various body shapes, or stressing selected parts of the body, or long springs or dives on to the hands, or off-balance jumps.

Up-spring jumps in which the take-off on apparatus increases the flight. Forms, inclined or flat, horses, boxes, storming boards, springboards and trampettes can be used. A single jump can be made, such as the traditional Jack-in-a-box, or a series of jumps, which make a rhythmic sequence. Many angles of approach should be tried as well as jumps in all directions and with turning. The take-off on the apparatus can be from various parts of the body as in a jump from shins or seat.

Vaults in which the arms support or push during the flight. This group includes most of the traditional vaults and there are three main types in which:

The body is carried over or round the arms in vaults such as crouch vault, front or flank vault and handspring.

The body is taken between the arms over apparatus placed crosswise as in the traditional squat vaults and thief vault, or, tiger leap over lengthwise apparatus.

One or both arms are used mainly to give added impetus to the flight as in leap frog or fence vault.

These vaults can be done as single actions, or as a series over: several pieces of apparatus such as three to four saddles on a bar, *or*

one piece used several times consecutively as when jumping many times over a horse, using all the spaces, i e both sides and centre.

The traditional vaults can be done in other than the accepted ways, e g a single start can be used rather than the traditional double start, and the legs need not go together but follow each other, or reach out wide apart, or be held in various positions during the flight. Squat vaults can be done with many different leg actions and with turning, direct from the start or during the flight, and they can be slowed down or greatly speeded up.

Assisted flight

In some actions the aim is to jump to grasp apparatus such as ropes, bars, wall bars, window ladders or rope ladders. At the first stage, to master the timing and get high up is in itself an absorbing task. Later, jumping from forms, bars or other apparatus on to stationary or swinging ropes is a further test of skill. Some youngsters need much practice before they achieve exactly the timing to leap and grasp at the right moment.

Interesting sequences can be constructed from leaping and swinging, such as leaping off apparatus to swing away, and at the farthest point land, roll and recover (or any other logical sequence of actions), in time to jump back on to the rope to swing home again to the starting point. Youngsters invent many exciting and intricate sequences based on leaping and swinging, and such actions can also be done as partner or group work. Flying, swinging movements are also used to carry the body over various obstacles, or lift it up on to bars, inclined forms, horses or boxes.

It is often necessary to coach the bodily and dynamic aspects of these actions. In the first stages, children often curl up as they jump to grasp the rope and cling close to it, and this is right in the initial stages and should be emphasised and encouraged. With more experience and skill a new development emerges, and they dare to leap and reach up and out, leaving the legs stretched out behind until, at the lowest point of the swing, the legs and body whip through to augment the upswing, with the whole body reaching out and away from the rope.

Other Assisted Flights are those in which a spring is made to grasp a bar or pole to increase the height and duration of the flight. A firm grasp and a quick, strong lift are needed to gain maximum height. These heave springs (the arms pull and bend) and swings (the arms are straight but pull from the shoulder) can be done as single actions such as jumping or swinging once through the bars, or as rhythmic repetitive jumps or swings using the bar many times in succession. Variation can be made by:

> Altering the angle of approach to the apparatus (facing, sideways or oblique).
> Changing the grip.
> Taking a double or a single start.
> Making a variety of leg movements during the flight.
> Twisting or turning (or both) in flight.

Forward heave swings can be dangerous because the legs and hips swing forward while the hands hold the weight back, and unless a weight adjustment is made to bring the body to vertical, there is risk of falling flat on the back. This can be avoided by making a strong twist at the height of the swing to turn the body to face the ground and land facing the place of take-off. The danger of falling on the back does not arise so easily in oblique swings in which the bar is grasped with one hand on each side of the bar. In a forward swing without any twist, the weight adjustment occurs at the height of the swing when the arms pull back slightly, while the legs swing down from the hips so that on releasing the bar, the leg movement rotates the body to the vertical ready for the landing (page 98). Some people find this a difficult adjustment to make and will need the teacher's help.

In all these flights and swings, the apparatus must be grasped very quickly and firmly and the grip must be held so that the hands, arms and shoulders are used with strength. The jolt of the weight suddenly falling on the arms may make the shoulders and body sag and this must be anticipated and counteracted. The big heaving muscles which envelop the chest, sides and back should take a firm hold and draw the body up towards the arms, which, at the same time, are pulled strongly down so that there is firm contact between the shoulder girdle and chest, with the head and neck drawn out of the shoulders, and no slackness or uncontrol in the hanging.

Many partner and group actions are forms of Assisted Flight. Two, three or more people can work together and help one another to jump, and they can give an exciting sensation of flying by holding the performer high above the ground. They can also help one another over or on to high apparatus, or catch people high up on a swinging rope and carry them off before lowering them to the ground. Good co-operation is imperative in these actions, and knowledge of lifting, carrying, supporting, lowering and placing are necessary (pages 69 and 79).

Flying through the air is the most exhilarating aspect of gymnastics and it is an important part of every lesson. More daring and intricate flight can be attempted as control and skill increase. Sometimes one sees classes of girls who do not seem to get beyond the stage of holding and clinging to the apparatus and so they do not experience any flight. Fear of being unsupported in the air and apprehension of the landing appear to be the chief inhibitory causes, and both of these can be alleviated by using various forms of Assisted Flight. The difficulties do not arise when well chosen challenges are given and if the training, from the beginning, has included wide experience of body management and movement as well as plenty of opportunity to use the apparatus.

Outline of progression

Lessons based on various aspects of Flight are suitable for every stage of skill and development. First year beginners particularly enjoy leaping and jumping and they should have plenty of opportunity to do so while they have the energy, enthusiasm and not too much weight. Children who do not leap and jump while they are small and light, often find it hard work and difficult, and resist it, at a later stage.

The most elementary work is concerned with receiving the weight, learning to land and recover, hopping and jumping to develop spring and good footwork, single and double starts for jumps from the floor or from low apparatus, and plenty of opportunity should be given to use the apparatus for jumping on to, over and off. Beginners must also have the chance to get high up, and this can be given through swinging on ropes, mounting inclined forms or climbing apparatus, as well as vaulting apparatus, for jumping down (on to thick mats) from heights chosen by themselves. Children should become competent in this type of activity before they use springboards or trampettes.

At an intermediate stage, further teaching is needed and practice given in take-off and landing, both for the maintenance and improvement of skill. Skill in building sequences of landing, rolling and recovering, or ways of taking the weight down to the ground, along it and away from it, gives the teacher opportunities for coaching all the points which help to make movement logical and give it greater fluency. Practices, without jumping, can be based on movements of the body such as those which are made during the flight, e g how and when to bend, stretch or twist, or what actions are made by the legs or arms, and which parts of the body are to be specifically stressed.

The dynamic changes which bring about the flight can also be clarified. Particularly important is the yielding to gravity on landing and fighting it in thrusting the body away from the ground. The different sensations of total yielding, and partial yielding which are experienced in the two main types of landing, should also be established. The changes in tension which are needed for taking, holding and releasing various body shapes are another aspect, and these should be experienced and practised with timings which might occur in the flight as 'effort training' (page 115).

There should also be more partner and group work of the type in which partners co-operate to help one another to jump. Higher apparatus can be used and there should be more vaulting and jumping right over the apparatus as well as jumping to balance upon it. At this stage of skill, trampettes can safely be used.

Progression to advanced school work could include any of the following:

Advanced work on trampettes, trampettes used with vaulting apparatus as well as using them in unorthodox ways and with approaches from all angles.

Flights combined with Balance, and actions which involve flying off-balance and recovering.

Any of the traditional vaults and heave springs and developments of these invented by the performers themselves.

The apparatus can be made more complex by the way it is arranged, with several pieces to use in succession, or one piece used many times without a break in the sequence. The skilled can use very high apparatus, and sensible people, both highly skilled and not so able, can be expected to make their own arrangements of apparatus. They also enjoy more intricate group work. At this high level of skill it is often fun to 'fool' with one's skill – clever clowning demands great skill – and through this people come back to the joy of 'play', having achieved the mastery which makes almost anything possible.

Themes

Several themes can be based on the concept of Flight but the work must not be composed only of leaping and jumping for this would be too strenuous in general, and in particular for the feet and legs. It is possible to give experience of matters relevant to flight without any jumping. This work would include how to control tension, increasing, decreasing and holding it, and how to touch the ground lightly (with various parts of the body) before transferring weight on to the part (pages 26 and 116). These skills are needed for safety in flight and landing. How to roll and get up on to the feet is necessary for fluent recoveries. To develop awareness and so improve the form of the flight itself can be done by stressing specific parts of the body in rising and sinking movements without getting off the ground.

Action themes

Receiving the weight.
Jumping, landing and recovering.
Flight.
Awareness of the body in flight.
Awareness of the legs in flight.
Flight combined with Balance.
Flight with On- and Off-balance.

ACTIONS EMPHASISING BALANCE

Some people are greatly disturbed by a loss of balance. Our daily lives lead us to adjust ourselves mainly to upright positions, and our eyes, ears and reflexes inform us when we are vertical. We get used to seeing the world right way up, with vertical and horizontal lines and surfaces, and everything which breaks this pattern may prove disturbing. Some people are upset when they see the world from upside-down, whizzing round or coming up at them as it may appear when they are falling. Experiences such as these are carefully introduced in gymnastics lessons, and learning to understand and cope with the balance of the body is a vital part of gaining control. As confidence grows the fears and discomforts associated with lost balance generally vanish.

The actions included in the group are:

Weight bearing.
Balancing Skills invented by the youngsters, and traditional skills such as headstands and balancing on the hands which are also generally discovered by experiment.

Actions of 'Arriving'. These actions have a double emphasis, to stop moving and to hold balance.

On- and *Off-balance* actions in which the body is launched away from the point of support to fly or tumble through space before it is caught and controlled, on-balance.

Actions in this group are an elementary form of Balancing Skills. The Weight Bearing activities stress mainly the parts of the body which touch the ground and support the weight and balance is only incidental. The main stress in Balance Actions is to gain, maintain and lose equilibrium, and there is more concern with the body as a whole balanced over a small base. The body is most stable when it is supported on a base covering a wide area as it is when supported on all fours, with knees and hands apart, or when lying down. Wide base stances are taken when stability is needed for supporting the weight of a partner or for strong pushing and pulling. It is much more difficult to hold balance when the area of support is narrowed or otherwise diminished, and balance is lost when the body moves so that the centre of gravity falls outside the supporting area. Movement through space is initiated when this happens, and it is arrested by checking and holding the body over the weight bearing parts.

Many surfaces can bear the weight of the body and in daily life this is practically confined to the feet for standing, the knees for kneeling, the hips for sitting, the trunk for lying and the hands for hanging. Weight is transferred when walking, rising from sitting to standing and similar everyday actions, but in gymnastics many other parts of the body bear weight either while the body is held on apparatus or the floor, or suspended from apparatus (bars, ropes, poles, rings). A great variety of agile actions come about by moving and stopping on all possible weight bearing parts, and skill in such bodily manipulations is necessary for the versatile activity of gymnastics. Body awareness is developed by weight bearing activities because the parts of the body touching the support can easily be felt pressing against it. In addition, the different positions held by the body in these activities stimulates the muscular feeling which is the main source of kinaesthetic awareness.

The first tasks related to weight bearing should be to discover all the parts of the body which will support the weight, and how the body must be adjusted to stay on the various bases, and how to move from one base of support to another. Children invariably try to take weight on many parts of the body, including shoulders and hips, parts of the thigh, knees, lower leg, forearms, hands or one hand, and the head. The next stage is to discover how to move smoothly over a series of bases, moving slowly or swiftly and with changes of direction. Experiments with the many ways of getting on to and off various parts of the body will be valuable when learning how to link sequences of movement in a logical way. Tasks for more experienced people can be to invent repeatable sequences in which the weight is held on a series of parts, e g successively on one foot, hips, shoulders, one knee and lower leg, one foot, and moved fluently from part to part. This is a form of 'stepping' (page 26), each part in turn prepares to receive the weight before it is placed ready for the weight change. The steps can vary in length, short if the receiving part is placed near the supporting part, and long when reaching or springing far out into position. If a class is prone to moving in a niggly, restricted manner, experimenting with the size of steps will bring more life and boldness, but the larger steps make the adjustments of the weight much more difficult. Ability to control the weight, moving continuously or with pauses, is often needed in apparatus work when moving across gaps from one height to another.

BALANCING SKILLS

Youngsters are generally interested in trying to balance themselves and they enjoy the experience of balancing on various parts of the body:

> Matching parts such as both hands or shoulders.
> Single parts such as one knee or one hand.
> Non-matching parts such as one foot and a forearm.
> Two or more parts supported on different levels.

The experience of weight bearing is an introduction to Balancing Skills, and progression is made by giving tasks which emphasise the balance element, by discovering ways of diminishing the base and balancing, as well as how to move from one position to another. After the first explorations more specific attention is given to the ways of transferring the weight into and out of position, and to the balance position itself. Rocking, rolling, various ways of 'stepping' and leaping are all possible ways of approaching a position of balance, and when the weight is to be unbalanced, it can be done either carefully by preparing and placing part of the body to receive it, or in more dashing ways by tilting over or by pushing away from the support or by taking away part of the base, and then tumbling down and rolling to another place. This type of experience is also needed for apparatus work where many sequences consist of moving towards the apparatus and balancing on it before toppling off to land and recover. The balance position itself depends on how the body is moved into position. The movement should lead to a final, clear body shape. Wide shapes come about by pressing away from the point of support and spreading out away from the centre of the body, and long ones by extending into a long line. Small compact shapes are made by gathering all parts to the centre, and twisted shapes are the result of screwing round it (page 92).

Clear and vivid movement depends on ability to control and feel the dynamic changes. Many people can sense how to adjust tension and bodily grip so that they can move and hold themselves as they intend, but those who have less good kinaesthetic sense can also be helped to master themselves through practices in which they concentrate on experiencing tension changes by feeling the pull, grip and release of muscles as they move. Practices should be invented by the teacher for this specific purpose. They should be very simple exercises so that no mechanical difficulties intrude to spoil the concentration on the dynamic changes. One example of how to do this is to start from a spread out position, lying on the floor. First the body is 'gathered' and presses up away from the ground so that the point of support is reduced by the lifting, until finally the body is lightly poised in a position of balance (on shoulders or hips or thigh or lower leg). The body must be held lightly while it is poised, and small, light, adjusting movements which should be consciously felt help to maintain equilibrium. Excess tension and exaggerated movements are common faults and must be corrected. In lowering the body slowly the feeling of getting a firm hold and gradually releasing tension can be experienced, and this can be contrasted with the sensation of letting go suddenly. Similar practices should be devised whenever necessary, to emphasise the need for dynamic changes and to give experience in making them. Quality of movement depends on this, therefore, skill in doing it is vital for full control. Any practices invented by the teacher for such special purposes should always be related immediately to the action for which they were designed. There is double value if people can be led to understand the underlying principles and the relation of the experience to other situations and not only the current one. Dynamic change is one of the common factors of movement and should, therefore, eventually be understood in this way.

Lessons based on Balancing Skills can easily become too slow and static but this can be counteracted by moving between positions of balance. If the transference of weight takes the body right away from the spot smoothly or with acceleration and deceleration, much more exciting sequences of movement can be made. The sequences should become rhythmically satisfying, and this depends on changes – moving and pausing, surging up and dying down – and the sequence must be logical if movement is to flow (pages 119 and 145).

ACTIONS OF 'ARRIVING'

The actions of 'Arriving' are interesting and challenging. They are, on the whole, more difficult than the Balancing Skills because greater control, quicker judgments and an unerring sense of balance are needed. One has to assess exactly where the weight bearing part (one or more) is to be placed, and to know precisely which this part is to be. The body weight must be steered so that the centre of gravity arrives over the base and is held there. Running and leaping, or swinging to arrive in a poised balance position needs skill and control. Forms, boxes or horses can be used for leaping to arrive on one foot, one knee, hips, or even the shoulders or the head, and swinging can lift the body to balance on bars in sitting, lying across the bar (on front, back or side) or standing poised above one or both feet. Fast movement often precedes the moment of arrival so the speed must be accurately judged, for too much momentum carries the weight beyond the vital point, and too little, fails to get it there. The latter is a more common fault with girls who may have to be encouraged to put more go and vigour into their efforts. These arrivals may be made either symmetrically or asymmetrically (page 94) or with simultaneous or successive movement. Simultaneous arrivals have a feeling of finality and stopping, whereas successive arrivals give a sensation of arriving gradually, ready to go on (page 96).

Losing balance in order to move out of position, can give exhilarating experience in the following ways:

By tilting off apparatus very slowly at first and with control.

By holding a rope (while poised on apparatus) and gradually falling on to it to be carried away by it.

By doing the same but with a twist to make the body spin while falling.

By jumping out into space to catch hold of a rope.

By a vigorous push to shoot away from the point of support.

The loss of balance can, however, be much more restrained and the recovery made through controlled ways of transferring weight. In all cases the recovery movement should continue to a natural end to make the action, as a whole, feel rhythmically complete.

Just as in the Balancing Skills, the first aim is to manage the body weight generally, but this alone is not enough and will not give satisfaction for long. Youngsters at secondary school stage of development want to know how to do things well, how to succeed in doing things elegantly and with skill and masterly control. Management of the movements of the body which give precision and form, and control of the dynamic changes which give quality to movement, become increasingly important.

ON- AND OFF-BALANCE ACTIONS

Balance tends to lead to stillness while loss of equilibrium induces motion through space. It is, however, possible to move from one place to another, virtually on-balance, by a constant change of the supporting base, as in many weight transferences and in balance walking where alternate legs are in position to receive the weight before it is transferred. But these actions are not being considered because On- and Off-Balance means something different, it is a play with body balance in which one dares to throw oneself out into space, or fall to the point of no return, and yet manage the situation so that control is regained and no damage done. Many adjustments must be made to catch the tumbling body and slow it down in rolling or other forms of weight transference. Balance can also be restored without falling by quick twisting movements to readjust the weight, or by rapid steps to catch up with the weight, or both these ways combined.

The preparatory movements which plunge the body off-balance can be adjusted according to courage and skill. Experiments in throwing the body on to a mat, at first from starting positions close to the floor and near the mat, can be stepped up by starting higher up and farther away, and finally by adding a run and spring which gives more momentum, so that the body is thrown and flies farther. To land, one tries to 'glide' towards and over the mat, touching down and moving on, in the way an aeroplane lands. Skilful judgment of the angle of touching down, and the swift weight transference while gaining control, prevent undue pressure on any part of the body, and are safety factors. Much practice is needed in these landings and people must become skilful before any wild or difficult flights are attempted.

The climax in these actions is the off-balance flight. Some feeling of being off-balance and flying through the air can be gained in a safe way through coming off the apparatus in the ways suggested in the previous section. Off-balance unsupported flights demand very skilful manipulation of the body, and courage. The thrusting away from the point of support, reaching into space, twisting, turning and adjusting the body during the flight, must all be managed, and so must the landing which follows. There are degrees of being off-balance. Even in a simple weight transference one may be momentarily off-balance – falling – until the new weight bearing part is placed, and this is also the case in many travelling actions. Many leaps and jumps while travelling may have elements of being

64

off-balance, for while moving through space, the body weight is unbalanced in order to go. The body can also be on-balance or off-balance in the air. When it is held symmetrically there is aerial balance which one sees in ski-jumping, aeroplanes or gliding gulls. The gymnastics actions of diving on to the hands, to land on both, depend on the symmetrical flight and balance in the air. It is much more exciting and demands greater skill and daring to leap, whirl and topple in asymmetrical, off-balance flights. This is advanced gymnastics and should only be attempted with people who are well in command of themselves. Teachers need to be sure that people are capable of very swift weight transferences, on feet, hands and feet, on the body, and in all these ways combined. They must not be afraid of high speed, and they must enjoy and be able to make very fast turning movements. They should be in full command of all types of landing and be able to adjust themselves instantly according to the way the weight is falling. These matters ensure their safety in recovery, which is the most difficult and tricky part.

Apparatus work

Every type of apparatus can be used and much of the work described in the section on Travelling (page 36) and Flight (page 51) can be exploited for actions which stress Balance. Slopes can be used for leaping on to, 'arriving' and arresting movement instantly, and tracks and circuits can be adapted so that movement is checked and held on some or each of the obstacles. Flight actions can be modified in the same way.

The apparatus work should include actions which emphasise:
Balance positions. The body can be supported and balanced on Danish bars, bars, poles, vaulting apparatus or forms. Forms can be used broad or narrow side up, on the level, inclined or moving. The actions should be phrased to include an approach to the apparatus, the balance position on it, and the recovery and movement away. The weight can also be suspended and balanced upside down or in other positions, on bars, wall bars, poles or window ladders.

Swinging or spinning while balancing is enjoyed by most people, and rings or ropes (one or two) or trapeze can be used. One ring gives excellent spinning experience and a trapeze can give varied opportunities for balancing on top of it or being suspended underneath it. In all these actions a variety of grips and supporting parts should be tried.

Sliding and spinning while balancing on any slippery surface is a way in which old and shiny apparatus or a slippery floor can be exploited. The balance can be made more difficult by reducing the weight bearing area. The propulsive force can be gravity (down slopes) or momentum given by the performer's own efforts of kicking or thrusting away, or pushing and pulling. A preparatory run will give momentum for sliding along or over apparatus. Quick turning movements will generate momentum for spinning, and partners can help to increase the duration of a spin or a slide. Apparatus which is mobile such as:

> level forms fixed between two rope ladders
>
> inclined forms fixed on ropes, rings or trapeze
>
> rolling apparatus

can also be used while sliding or spinning and for Balancing Skills, but they must be used with great caution for it is much more difficult to keep control when the supporting apparatus is unstable.

'Arriving' on apparatus should stress either stopping or balancing. The approach to the apparatus can be by:

> Travelling or weight transference.
>
> Running and jumping.
>
> Swinging on ropes, rings or other hanging apparatus.

When the point of the action is to arrive and stop, the whole body lands simultaneously. Generally a wide and stable base is placed and the arrival is quick and firm. If balance is to be emphasised, only a small area of the body touches, and the arrival can be made with simultaneous or successive movement. The climax of such actions is the moment when the lightly poised body is held in a clear shape.

Off-balance falls and leaps using hanging apparatus to hold or grasp can give experience in falling (with support) or flying (to catch hold) but without the difficulties or dangers of the landings in unsupported actions.

Vaults and jumps on to, hurtling over or away from apparatus can be made to stress off-balance moments in the take-off or the flights, and free jumps from springboards or trampettes are an exhilarating way to fly and tumble – off balance.

Outline of progression

Lessons based on the concept of Balance interest people at all stages of skill. The most elementary material is concerned with weight bearing, and progress is made from this to the simplest balancing skills and ways of moving from one position to another. Later in the elementary stage more attention must be paid to ways of moving into and away from balance positions, and to the precision of the positions themselves. People enjoy swinging to arrive on apparatus, at all stages, and at the elementary level this type of activity can be done in simple ways stressing weight bearing rather than precise positions.

Both in the intermediate and advanced stages people continue to be interested in Balancing Skills which can always be a challenge. Repeatable sequences of movement, both for floor work and apparatus work, give the teacher a chance to coach and the class a chance to practise in order to acquire greater precision as well as skill in phrasing movement. All forms of 'Arriving' are absorbing provided the challenges have been well chosen and this is partly because people can so easily assess their own success or failure. Some of the preparatory work for 'On- and Off-balance' may prove suitable. Physically, people may well be able to cope, but at the adolescent stage which, in any case, may be one of unbalance, it may be more helpful to them to develop work which stresses stability and control.

All forms of Actions emphasising Balance can be exploited as advanced gymnastics as there is no limit to the challenges which can be created and the skill which must be exercised. More understanding should be evident, of the relevancy of simultaneous and successive ways of moving in the Skills of Arriving (page 96), and appropriate quality and subtler rhythms might be expected Daring on- and off-balance actions can be attempted, with or without apparatus and as partner or group work.

At all stages partner and group work should play a part. The least experienced enjoy coaching each other with the teacher's guidance. Matching movements and actions in which partners help one another to balance are also suitable. At the next stage partners invent more actions in which they balance upon each other and they find out ways of counterbalancing one another's weight. Those who have had considerable experience and are skilled, balance each other in much more intricate skills such as lifting, carrying and throwing each other, or catching people tumbling off apparatus, or catching flying partners. Many more ways of counterbalancing a partner's weight are invented at this stage.

Action Themes

Weight bearing and weight transference.

Control of body weight.

Balance and weight transference.

Balance Actions and Body Awareness.

'Arriving'.

'Arriving' combined with simultaneous and successive body movement.

Balance combined with Flight.

On-balance and Off-balance.

On- and Off-balance with Flight.

HANDLING

The handling of apparatus is part of every gymnastics lesson. Portable apparatus has to be lifted, carried and placed, and fixed apparatus is pushed or pulled into position. There is danger of strain unless people are taught how to lift, carry, push and pull, and these are actions which do not come naturally to most people, which is a reason for teaching them definite techniques. Faulty habits established in childhood are carried on and then as adults the price has to be paid in fibrositis, slipped discs and strains. Experts, who have made careful study of these matters, have devised techniques for handling objects of various sizes and shapes, and there is a wealth of written material and films available which give detailed information and, therefore, only bare outline facts will be given here.

Lifting, carrying and placing

Practice and knowledge of sound techniques for lifting, carrying and placing can be given in gymnastics lessons through the moving of forms, horses, boxes, agility mattresses and smaller pieces of individual apparatus. The main danger to guard against in lifting and carrying is back strain and this can be avoided if the handling is done in an efficient way. The main points to stress are that:

The whole body should participate in the action even when lifting and handling small and light things.

The preparation for lifting is made by getting close to the apparatus and lowering the hips. The object must be grasped firmly and in a balanced way.

The stance should give good balance and make it easy to move with the apparatus, therefore, the feet are placed apart, one in front of the other and in line with the direction of movement.

The work of lifting must be done mainly by the legs and hips, therefore the body weight is lowered by bending the knees and taking the hips down, and then the legs, hips and lower trunk are braced, ready for lifting with firmness and strength.

The body weight should be moved beneath the object as soon as possible so that the whole body can participate in pushing vertically upwards through the legs, hips and trunk.

The back must be firm and nearly vertical but without inflexible rigidity, and with readiness to adjust for any emergency. The head is held up to help the straight back position, and so that the eyes can be used for looking where to go.

The arms and shoulders are firmer and steadier if the arms are supported against the body. When carrying things with a partner, the arms are generally held nearly straight for economy of effort (a slight flexion of the elbow takes the strain off the joint). When the things being carried have to be held higher up, there is least strain on the arms and shoulders if the elbows are bent up to right angles or higher.

Smaller, lighter objects are handled in the same way but as there is less weight, less power is needed. The whole body should, however, share in the lifting and moving of even the lightest things. It may appear to be a waste of energy to take the hips right down to lift a hoop off the ground, but when this is done incorrectly, with straight legs, energy is used wastefully and in the wrong way to fix parts of the body, and the work is thrown mainly on the back. When the whole body works as a unit every part takes a share of the work and nothing is strained. Strain from faulty ways of lifting and carrying may be cumulative and not immediately apparent, and experts who have studied working techniques maintain that it is just as important to handle light things in the right way, a way which incorporates the whole body in the action.

Pushing and pulling

Bars, ropes and window ladders often have to be pulled into position and apparatus on rollers, pushed or pulled. Strength and firmness is needed in the whole body for pushing and pulling heavy objects. The firmness and strength come from the grip on the ground and the dynamic tension in the legs, hips and lower back. The trunk as a whole must be active, the back firm but movable, and the whole body adjusting to keep in line with the direction of the pushing or pulling. The feet should be apart and in line with the direction of movement, and in pushing, the rear leg is braced and pushes against the ground so that the thrust is in the direction of moving, while the front leg is flexed and acts mainly to give stability and balance. In pulling, the front leg thrusts and the rear leg stabilises. For balance, the hips must be kept over the area of the supporting base, and so that the body weight can be used effectively in the action, the hips and trunk must be held in line with the thrusting leg. (To apply more weight in heavy pushing and pulling the weight is moved beyond the supporting base). Even much lighter pushing and pulling should be done by using the body weight in the action, and not only by pulling with the arms.

Managing partners is another aspect of handling and there are more problems to contend with when handling people. They move, change shape and may do the unexpected, so the helpers must be very adaptable. Before allowing people to lift and carry one another, the teacher must be sure that the children are strong enough, have had enough preparatory experience, are adaptable and used to working with partners. The ways of handling people are discussed in the section on Partner and Group Work.

Development of skill in handling apparatus

The handling of apparatus is important for not only is it an exercise in co-operation, it is also a lesson in the competent management of a variety of objects. Efficiency in this respect is proof of skill and understanding of the use of movement for truly practical purposes. The training in lifting and carrying also has value for everyday tasks and the teacher must ensure that this is appreciated by the class.

The techniques for lifting, carrying, placing, pushing and pulling should be put into practice from the very beginning of gymnastic experience. Beginners can merely be shown and frequently reminded, what to do, until good habits are formed. Intelligent children will probably soon ask why things should be done in this way, and when they do, this is the time to explain and give reasons. The question should be taken up again with school leavers so that they can go away with sound knowledge of useful techniques which they will need in their post-school life.

Repetition is important in training beginners to handle different types of apparatus. Each group should learn in turn how to get out and put away such things as bars or boxes, and they need to handle the same things for several consecutive lessons in order to establish ways of doing it skilfully. It is also advisable in the initial stages of introducing a new theme for groups to get out and put away the same apparatus. This saves time in the next lesson because the group which first arranged a set of apparatus is more likely to remember exactly where it is to be placed as well as the heights and relationship of things, and they will, therefore, be more competent in getting it ready. There is doubtful value in practising getting the apparatus out and putting it away without using it as this generally irritates and disappoints the children. Even less useful is the practice of going round all the apparatus to show a beginner class how to handle everything. The children must handle it themselves, and use it, before it becomes a real and useful experience to them. They will not learn only by watching.

In some of the early lessons with beginners, practice can be given in which apparatus (forms, mats, small boxes) is carried, placed with care and with good spacing, and used freely until a new signal is given to pick it up, move it to a new place and put it down again. Partners must be taught to watch one another, do things together and help each other in every way. In this way much experience and practice of lifting, carrying and placing, can be given. Youngsters can learn to move very nimbly in and out or swirling round each other, without collisions or mishaps while carrying apparatus. They also become more adept in watching and judging the spacing and much time is saved in lessons if apparatus handling is done efficiently. Moving about while carrying apparatus is tiring and should not be overdone; frequent short practices are much more effective than a few long and tiring turns. Material such as this is appropriate in connection with themes on Locomotion.

Beginners should, however, always be urged to move apparatus with care rather than speed, whereas competent, well trained classes should be expected to do it both carefully and speedily. Crashing and banging are caused by carelessness, lack of thought and unawareness and it is possible to learn to judge exactly when contact will be made (forms with floor, bars with pegs) and to control how it is done. Youngsters enjoy doing things well and efficiently, particularly if the teacher shows appreciation, and it is possible to become highly competent in handling apparatus.

When the apparatus is taken out for the Section Work, everyone should look at the spacing and be helped to consider what may happen when the apparatus is used. They must be taught to look that everyone has room to move, that ropes will not swing into other sections, that people have room to approach and land, and that those waiting for turns are not in anyone's way. Sometimes a slight adjustment of some apparatus, or a changed direction of approach is all that is necessary to make everyone more comfortable. Checking the safety of the apparatus is ultimately the teacher's responsibility, but the youngsters should be trained to be aware, sensible and responsible. The teacher can foster the attitude that class and teacher are jointly responsible for the safety of all. The class can become interested in checking things for security, both in their own section and anything they happen to see elsewhere, and this applies before the apparatus work starts, as well as in the course of the lesson. Attention must be drawn to anything which might slip or tip, and advice and reminders of how to cope with it should be given. On the whole people should not be allowed to alter the position of apparatus without the teacher's knowledge. The teacher should explain why this must be so; that it has been planned to give everyone room and ensure their safety, and that difficulties arise for the teacher through not knowing exactly what is happening. The apparatus should never be used in ways not intended by the manufacturers, horses and bucks should not be put down on one side and the legs used for vaulting or other forms of supporting weight. The legs of this apparatus are carefully balanced with a series of small wedges, and they are able to take any amount of weight and remain steady but only when used in the way intended. Apparatus on rolling gear, unless specially constructed, is not meant to take more weight than the apparatus itself, so no one should be allowed to ride on it or use it in a rolling position. Routine, humdrum work of this kind carried out well is a clear indication to the teacher of the growing awareness and sense of responsibility of the class as well as the development of self-discipline.

PARTNER AND GROUP WORK

Much of the action in gymnastics is individual; people work in their own time, interpret in their own way and progress according to their own ability. Nevertheless, every gymnastics lesson is essentially a group activity because the aim is to reach a stage where everyone contributes to the lesson, shares with the teacher and fellow pupils, helps everyone, cares for the safety, ease and confidence of others, and all jointly, make the lessons go.

Partner and group work are excellent ways of giving people a chance of working together, which they greatly enjoy, and at the same time extending their movement experience in new ways. Working together entails adapting to someone else, sharing with them, planning, arranging, selecting and experiencing things together. Observation and critical powers are developed through watching, helping and constructively criticising one another. Partnerships and groups are used in the floor work and the apparatus work and both can range from elementary to highly advanced. There should be some partner or group work in every lesson at secondary school stage. In halls where there is little equipment, partner and group actions can be a substitute for apparatus work, but it can by no means ever satisfactorily take the place of it.

Generally it is wise to allow people to choose their own partners and groups, friends enjoy working together, but there are many factors to consider which the teacher must help the children to understand. In partner work some actions require people of equal size and weight, whereas in others, this factor need not be taken into account, and there are occasions when it is perfectly possible for a small, light child to work with a big, heavy one. Big, heavy children often make excellent, sensitive helpers, and they get great satisfaction from this, and provided both partners have an exacting part to play, it is not always necessary for them to change roles in the partnership. The teacher must help them to understand how best they can aid one another. Sometimes an able child can work with one less able; at other times it is wiser to stretch the highly skilled by pairing them and demanding work from them commensurate with their ability. Similarly, the less able are often happier working together in their own way and in their own time. A class with a good group feeling will readily understand the value of working with a variety of different people and will willingly change their grouping according to need.

Partner work

Partners can work together with or without touching one another, and naturally the actions with contact demand greater interdependence than those without, and on the whole, they are a more advanced type of work. Movement experience is extended in various ways by the different types of partner work.

Actions without contact

Matching, mirroring, follow-my-leader

These are the types of action in which partners make exactly the same movements. The value of such partnerships is that new movement experiences are opened up since the rhythms and patterns of other people's movement are felt. People also learn to give and take and experience what it is like to lead and to follow. They often have to decide together what to do, and adaptations have to be made to accommodate the skill and interests of both. Both must observe accurately if the rhythm, timing and shaping of actions is to coincide. Much practice and repetition is necessary if accuracy is to be achieved and this means that movement memory is developed because they must remember what to do. Sometimes one partner teaches the other, and when this can be done by demonstration, without talking (this can be made a condition of the task), the 'teacher' must make very clear and consistent demonstrations while the 'pupil' must be equally observant and perceptive. When talking is used as a means of teaching, the 'teacher' should be encouraged and helped to use few words and to express clearly what is required to get the 'pupil' moving as soon as possible, and to give constructive criticism and encouragement. Interested and lively children respond to being given such responsibility.

Adapting to partners

Other types of elementary partner work are games in which partners adapt to one another going over, under or round one another, or through holes formed by one for the other to negotiate. (Holes are formed by enclosing an area of space by standing with the legs apart, by standing on all fours lifting away from the ground, or by using apparatus, e g holding or placing a foot on the wall bars.) Going through the holes and round the 'pillars' should be done without touching and with continuity of movement.

More difficult actions are those in which one partner makes and holds a body shape (long, wide, curved or twisted) while the other goes over or under making a similar shape or a directly contrasting one. The performer must be observant, adaptable and able to make quick decisions. The 'obstacle' should be expected to show consideration and ability to assess the partner's skill, as well as ingenuity to make the game fun and exciting. Better judgment is needed if both partners move at the same time, the 'obstacle' changing shape and moving on the floor, while the partner adapts by going over, under or round as the situation demands. In another version of the game the role of obstacle and performer is alternated as when one jumps over a rolling partner, who then gets up and gets ready to jump, while the leaper lands and gets down in time to be jumped over.

At the experimental stage such actions may be a scramble, but with repetition and practice they should build up into logical sequences of movement. The finished product should be composed so that there is a beginning, a middle and an end. There should be a clear starting situation. The climax of the action is the moment of negotiating the partner, and preparatory movements lead to this point, while the recovery movements follow the climax. Single phrases such as these should be linked together into a continuous sequence, and this means paying special attention to the way of making the links. Often the recovery phase after one climax merges with the preparation for the next action, and this continues until the sequence ends in a final position, after the last recovery is completed. The performer's last recovery is often a signal for partners to change role – while it is happening the 'obstacle' gets ready for a turn while the performer, as part of the recovery, becomes the obstacle. People enjoy composing such sequences as they give a sense of completeness and make a satisfying whole (page 119).

Actions with contact

The actions in which partners touch and handle one another need greater dependence on each other than the types already described. The actions include ways of supporting, counterbalancing, pushing, pulling, lifting, carrying, placing, catching and throwing partners. The points made for the handling of apparatus (page 69) should be applied for handling partners, but a living partner is less predictable than inanimate apparatus and, therefore, a greater readiness to adapt is necessary. Some of the ways in which partners (one or two) can work together are:

One supports the other.

Two contest with each other.

Partners counterbalance one another's weight.

One or more help a partner to jump.

One or more lift, carry or catch a partner.

One supports the other

To be a supporter it may only be necessary to keep firm and act as a reliable piece of apparatus for the partner to balance upon or vault over. The supporter's base must give stability and good balance, and it must be adjusted in line with the direction from which the partner (the force) is coming. The whole body must be braced so that there is no sagging or collapsing when the partner exerts pressure. The performer must show consideration by grasping, leaning or taking off in a way which will not hurt the supporter. Sometimes the supporter is more active and holds or helps the performer to balance. The supporter can take up a variety of starting positions, and the performer balance, with help, in many different positions and on various weight bearing parts.

Many ways of wheeling over partners are possible and the supporter can use various starting positions such as lying on the back with legs ready to take the performer's weight, or standing in a firm lunge position (legs wide apart with the weight over a firm, bent leg and with a firm, straight supporting leg) ready to help the performer. It is important to know where to give support. This is often at the hips, by the performer's centre of gravity, as this gives the supporter the best chance of controlling the performer's weight. The helper must first catch, then take, then guide the performer's weight towards the place of the landing. The performer must also be active. The grasp and placing of weight bearing parts must be accurate, all movements well timed and predictable and the body firm enough for the supporter to be able to keep control of it.

Two contest with each other

Contests based on pushing, pulling and wrestling also demand an understanding of how to adjust and vary firmness and strength in movement in order to handle and counteract an external resistance. Games such as wrestling to turn over a partner lying on the floor, give both partners a vivid experience of tension changes in the body. Each feels the resistance and pressure of the other, and the sudden changes on releasing a hold. They also feel the resistance and power they must generate in themselves, and they can be taught to brace the trunk and all parts of the body in turn, as they are needed for the game. In the actual game attention is naturally absorbed by the game itself, but people can become aware of how to use their powers. In order that attention can be given wholly to the feeling of strong muscular tensions affecting the trunk and transferring to other parts of the body, opportunity should be taken, when such games are played, for giving short spells of effort training. Strong, firm, twisting in all parts of the body can first be contrasted with the feeling of slack, quality-less movement. Later it is more effective to contrast the firm movements of the main actions with the lighter movements which are made in the preparation. The younger children enjoy shadow wrestling, near but not touching a partner. This approaches drama, but if attention is focused on experiencing and sensing how to change the power in various parts of the body, it is a way of gaining conscious control and ability to make the tension changes which are a vital part of effective gymnastics.

In pushing and pulling contests, many different ways of holding each other or pressing against one another should be tried. Tests of various foot and leg positions should be made which result in discovering the need for a firm grip on the ground and springy resilience in the legs. The most effective body and hip position should be found and tested so that efficient use can be made of the body weight. Both in strong pushing and pulling, the feet should be apart and firmly gripping, and the weight should fall over the bent leg. The hip should be in line between the trunk and the straight leg which thrusts against the ground. The power must be transmitted through the leg and hip to the trunk, so that the body weight and the power of the body can be used effectively. Much power is lost if the hip 'hinges' and slips out of line (page 70).

Partners counterbalance one another's weight

This is closely related to pushing and pulling but judgment is required to exert a specific degree of power which will exactly counteract a partner's weight. Partners can lean or pull against each other and in this manner walk, spin round, side step, change places, lower or raise themselves. Each must deal with the other's weight and adapt to it by yielding or resisting. They must lean towards or away from each other so that their own centre of gravity is well outside their own supporting base, and, to avert collapse, they are compelled to rely entirely on the counterweight of the partner. It is not essential for partners to be the same weight for unless the discrepancy is very great, it is possible to adjust to one another. After experimenting and experiencing the effect of both leaning and pulling, with many different ways of grasping each other, these actions can be built up into skilful, exciting sequences of movement, both on the floor and using apparatus. The beginning of any sequence consists of the two coming together and taking each other's weight, and then they move and act as one and are totally reliant upon one another. The action can be ended by breaking away from each other, followed by individual movements consequent to the breaking, or it can be ended more calmly by each pushing or pulling the other one back to personal balance. The children's game of spinning in twos and breaking to make statues, is an unsophisticated version of an action ending in a break away.

It is a different feeling if one partner yields with control so that the other one slowly falls. As in the game 'weighing salt' the lowering can be done alternately, or it can be used as a controlled way of lowering a partner to the floor or even down from apparatus. The opposite action, using the weight to pull a partner up from the ground can be used to start or end many different sequences of movement. Done calmly it will bring the partner up to balance, and done quickly and energetically, it can give momentum to start jumping, spinning and other fast movement.

One or more help a partner to jump

Both the actions of the helper (one or two) and of the performer have to be considered. The performer's aim is to get much higher and stay up longer than is possible without help, and the helper's purpose is to make this happen. The moment of the take-off is all important for it is then that the main help is given. At this moment the helper must be stationary to be able to give a strong upward thrust from a firm base. The supporter should, therefore, first learn to lift from a stationary stance which is close to the place of the take-off. The stance is with feet apart and in line with the direction from which the leaper is coming. The supporter must be firm and ready to adjust to the weight of the partner who comes with considerable momentum. The performer is grasped and lifted at the moment of the take-off while the body is rising, to help it to rise more. The actual executive movement has to be very quick and strong, but it must be judged accurately so that the performer is not thrown off-balance by the action. If the helper can maintain a strong upward pressure, the flight can be prolonged and the landing slowed down. More skill is needed to lift and release the leaper so that the high flight and the landing have to be made without help. These are exciting partner jumps for those who are skilled enough to manage them.

The leaper must also be skilful. The take-off must be made in the right place, close to the helper, and at the right moment. There must be a way of judging exactly when the take-off will be made, and the clue for this is the rhythm of the run and the take-off which the helper must be able to anticipate. The momentum gained by the running approach must be changed from a forward to an upward direction to coincide with the helper's thrust which also will be upward to give height to the jump. The force can only be transmitted through a firm body, therefore, the leaper must fly up strongly and hold the firmness in the flight. Too early release of tension makes difficulties for the helper who then has to deal with a slack and heavy partner.

The helper can grip the performer in various ways, by the arms, the waist, thorax or hips, or even with an asymmetrical hold such as one arm and the side of the thorax, and the performer must adjust in order to get the best effect from the help. When the performer's arms are free they should be used to aid balance or to augment the flight by pressing on the helper's shoulders or other convenient place. When the help is given through the arms, both helper and performer must judge and time the movements accurately. The most functional grasp must first be discovered. A very usual grip is for the helper's arms to be forward, bent at the elbows with palm up. The performer grasps the helper's forearm at the elbow, while the helper also takes a firm grip and both push hard against each other as the leaper flies up. The commonest faults in pair jumping are that the partners are too far apart at the take-off (the helper cannot get beneath the performer for lifting), the performer jumps at or past the helper (through failure to redirect the take-off), and the moment of thrusting is mistimed.

When the jumps are done on the run, the helper must make a momentary check for the take-off. This is because the high upward movement delays the forward rush, but more important, because a firm stance is needed for making an effective, strong lifting movement. Many of these jumps can be done with two helpers and it is often easier for the performer than having only one, but the two helpers must be able to co-operate in their lifting for each is responsible and help must be given equally by both.

Partners can help one another to jump on to and off apparatus, and apparatus can be used for the take-off. This makes the helping easier in one way as the performer gets high with much less help, but it is also more difficult because of the added height of the jump which demands more care and judgment from the helper.

Sequences of movement can be composed using this type of material. A sequence should have an appropriate starting position, an approach, take-off and jump, landing and recovery movements which lead either to a change of role, or to a repetition. One partner can jump several times before a change is made, but all movement, including the changeover, must be part of the whole, and a way of ending the sequence should also be found.

One or more lift, carry or catch a partner

Even Fireman's lift or riding on a partner should be done with awareness of the proper ways of lifting and carrying. Various other games also give good experience of this, e g two carriers can run towards and sweep a partner off the ground and without pause, run on or spin round, and then finish the phrase by releasing the third, without any break in the movement. Two helpers can find ways of swinging a third, but sensible ways of stopping the swing and releasing the partner must also be discovered. Many ingenious solutions can be found but a clear warning must be given to hold tight and to take care. Such games should not be allowed unless the teacher is convinced that the class is fully competent.

Other ways can be invented in which one or more helpers lift, carry and place a partner. More advanced skills are those in which a partner, leaping or swinging on a rope is 'caught' and then carried away to be put down, or 'flung' away. These actions also demand very good team work and reliability from every member of the group. They should not be attempted unless people are fully capable of good co-operation and have considerable movement experience as well as plenty of practice in simpler ways of lifting and carrying. Everyone should be so versatile and adaptable that they know how to save themselves, and others, if anyone falls.

Group work

Group work has the same purpose and qualities as partner work but it is more advanced. At a certain stage, people show eagerness to work together and through group work they are able to do this. They are helped by it to develop more understanding and tolerance of one another. They become more interested in the ideas and efforts of other people since all are helped, by the group, to find a role which is suitable for their capabilities. Group work often arises spontaneously; a group at apparatus suddenly starts working together, matching or interweaving, and when this happens, it is a clue to the teacher that the class is ready for this step. It is generally advisable to keep groups small, three to five people, and group work is possible both with and without apparatus.

The tasks and challenges must be carefully chosen and worded so that the group is stimulated to move rather than talk. Much time can be wasted in talking, which is necessary, but in moderation. Well trained youngsters more often are able to show what they mean, instead of explaining in words, and this is to be encouraged. Another problem which arises is that people do not use their skill to the full. They become so intent on fitting in with others that little thought can be spared for the way of moving. This should be remedied as soon as the group becomes familiar with the intricacies of their joint action. They should be helped to keep their ideas simple and with logical development. This is most likely to happen if the group experiments practically, finding step by step what can happen next. Group work easily becomes contrived and this should be avoided.

Some of the actions with partners are, strictly speaking, Group Work since three or more people co-operate together and all are needed for the successful execution of the action. Much of the work suggested as Partner Work can become Group Work. The simplest form of Group Work is in actions without contact such as:

Matching, mirroring, follow-my-leader

The whole group carries out the same action, moving simultaneously or successively, or in various other patterns. Many different formations can be used. Timing and rhythm are important in these actions.

Adaptations to one another

Moving in a restricted space stimulates all in the group to adapt spontaneously to each other by moving over, under, round one another in leaping, landing, rolling or balancing. Quick adaptations, awareness of other people's movement, awareness of space and anticipation are needed for this type of action.

Actions with contact demand greater reliance on others and the ability to work as one of a team. The type of work includes many actions similar to those described as Partner Work:

Some support while others move (page 77).

Counterbalance (page 78). A group can find ways of counter-balancing each other and there is scope for two or more to lower and raise 1–3 partners as in 'weighing salt'.

Two or more help others to jump (page 79).

Two or more people lift, carry or catch a partner (page 81).

Apparatus work

Many of the ideas with or without contact can be used. Typical examples are:

Building patterns using apparatus such as window ladders or double bars. A group, all working together move up, down, along, through, lean away and pull in to the apparatus, interweaving and making kaleidoscope patterns.

Interchanging using horses, boxes or a combination of apparatus to get on to, off and over, with or without help from others, inter-changing and timing the actions to fit in together while all work at the same time.

Matching one another's movement using:
Single bars for actions such as a succession of body waves under the bar.

Rope swings to arrive on and swing away from bars.

Rhythmic jumps on or along bars.

Heave springs (jumps with pulling on apparatus) to and fro between double bars.

These actions can be made simultaneously by the whole group or successively, and in a variety of other patterns.

Lifting, carrying and catching partners using high apparatus to help one another on to, off and over it and to catch partners flying on ropes, or falling off apparatus.

Counterbalancing one another to lower partners from apparatus or lift them up on to it.

A group in which all members have roughly the same ability may also be interested in:

Stream Vaults in which a regular, fast follow-on is maintained, either everyone doing exactly the same as the leader
or, selecting individual actions, but keeping the rhythm going.

Follow-my-leader vaulting, jumping or travelling.

The last two suggestions are not Group Work in the truest sense because each person acts independently and only adapts to the group for the rhythm and timing. The actions do, however, interest able groups and they are a test of adaptability, nimbleness and agility.

A final warning must be given. Group Work is greatly enjoyed by people who have had enough experience and skill to exploit it, but unless this is the case, it can be a waste of time and a travesty of what it should be, and may degenerate into aimless drifting and cause discipline problems. Groups must always be kept small so that everyone is working and no one stands aside and feels left out.

MOVEMENT

Included in this section are three aspects of movement:

Bodily aspects.

Dynamic aspects.

Spatial aspects.

BODILY ASPECTS OF ACTION

Body awareness

Body awareness involves sensing how any part of the body is moving and the effect this has on the body as a whole. Awareness in this sense means knowing-by-feeling rather than intellectual knowledge, though this may be needed at certain stages in the learning process. The body should always be used as a unit, but in all actions, parts of it carry out special functions, while the whole reacts and adjusts to take a share in whatever is being done. In leaping there is obvious need for vitality and awareness in the use of feet, legs and hips to project the body into the air, and also to be ready to receive the weight, with fine precision, on landing. The poise of the body as a whole and movements made during the flight also affect the issue and necessitate an awareness of the whole and all the parts which contribute to the action.

Young children sense intuitively how to use the body as a unit, and all parts seem to be vitally alive, but by secondary school stage, this sense has often become dulled and some people show very little signs of *kinaesthetic* awareness. This may be due to the physically inactive lives which many children lead. Their earlier movement awareness does not develop fully through lack of use and, therefore, in order to re-awaken and restore awareness it may be necessary to rehabilitate the body. Conscious control of movement seems to restore and develop kinaesthetic sense, and it may have to be exercised in the first stages of learning any skilled action, but as soon as possible, the general feeling of the action should be established, and when it is, there is less need for conscious thought. Thinking and analysing tend to disrupt and disintegrate the rhythm of action, and movement should, in the long run, be felt, rather than thought, therefore, children should be encouraged to feel movement rather than be exhorted to think what they are doing. The mind is used to help the body but not to take command for one does not understand movement except through the body.

Skill in body management is developed through:

Bending and stretching.

Twisting and turning.

Making body shapes.

Symmetric and asymmetric movements.

Simultaneous and successive movements.

Swinging and circling.

Movements emphasising special parts of the body.

Bending and stretching

Bending, stretching and twisting are the fundamental movements of the body and they occur continuously as we move. Our anatomical structure, with movable joints, enables us to contract the whole body to make it more compact, or stretch it and thereby lengthen or spread it. The movements of bending and stretching are clearly seen in actions such as curling up close to a bar to somersault round it and stretching out to stand up again. Bending is needed for ducking under low things or for shooting through small spaces, and stretching is stressed in high leaps, or long dives on to the hands, or in reaching to grasp high bars, and in many actions with weight on hands. But if skill is to be improved in actions such as high leaps or cartwheeling, it may be necessary to change the focus of attention from the general aims, and concentrate more specifically on the movements of the body. Greater awareness can be developed by means of movement experience in which attention is clearly focused on aspects of bending and stretching, and this will eventually bring greater clarity and precision in action.

Development of bending and stretching

The centre of the body, the whole central region of the trunk, is the focal point for movement. The process of drawing in and extending out from the centre, should be experienced kinaesthetically. Bending relates to gathering the whole body, including the upper and lower parts of the trunk itself, towards the central region, while stretching means moving all parts out and away from the middle of the body. The pelvis and lower end of the spine always work with the hips and legs, and the head, chest and upper spine with movements of the shoulders and arms. The central region moves with both the lower and upper parts of the body thus uniting the whole body in harmonious movement. The head and neck move with the upper spine, and the eyes generally follow the main direction of movement as this helps to integrate everything and gives a more purposeful feeling. The structure of the spine allows bending, stretching and twisting in every direction towards the central region and out into the Personal Space surrounding the body (page 126). Youngsters should be encouraged to become just as adept in arching backward, twisting and bending sideways, as they are in bending forward. All these movements are essential for versatility and plasticity in movement, and in addition, they are important in developing strength and suppleness. The co-ordination and vitality of the body are also increased, so, for all these reasons, movement which concentrates on the trunk, should form part of every lesson. Bending and stretching need not be only spoke-like movements to and from the centre, they can also be carried round the body, near it or far away, and such curving peripheral movement can link the outgoing and incoming movement and it may also take the body into travelling or flight, or into turning and spinning.

The positions which are reached by going to the limits of both bending and stretching should be felt as well as intermediate positions. Positions should always be sensed as a vital state, as if movement were reined in, ready to be released to start again. All parts of the body participate in moving into and out of positions as well as holding them. The stretched shape at the climax of some jumps is achieved by an energetic, quick stretching of the whole body whereas the uncurling to stand balanced on the head is probably done much more slowly and gently. The final positions, in both cases, must be held actively and released appropriately, at a chosen moment. Positions like the rounded forms for rocking or rolling must also be taken and held, with awareness, if skill and precision are to be achieved.

Ability to feel the sensation of curling inward in contrast with stretching outward, as well as the moment of changing from one to the other, gives control of the flow of movement and mastery of such changes. The moment of change from holding a position to moving again should also be made with awareness, as the exact timing in many skills depends on controlling moments such as these when something new starts (pages 113 and 120).

Lessons based on this material should give experience in these aspects of bending and stretching which should be thoroughly explored (pages 134ff).

Tasks should include:

Gymnastic actions on floor and apparatus including locomotion, jumping and balance, which clearly show the need
for bending and stretching.

Movements which concentrate on the experience of bending
and stretching and in which the following ideas are stressed:

Use of many different weight bearing parts

Speed and tension changes

Use of many directions

Taking, holding and releasing positions

Movements which lead, through extra extension, to weight
transference, travelling and flight

Continuous movement contrasted with movement broken
by pauses

The many apparently non-functional movements which some
people would argue do not belong to gymnastics, are a 'tuning'
process which makes the body more manageable and deft. Some of
the floorwork and all the apparatus work consists of gymnastic
actions which demand skilful manipulation of the body. This appli-
cation, together with the teacher's explanations, should clarify why
such understanding and skill are necessary, and as people become
more experienced, they also have the satisfaction of getting greater
mastery of themselves.

Twisting (and turning)

(Turning is not a fundamental body movement but it has a close
affinity with twisting and, therefore, they are described together.)

Twisting, bending and stretching are the three possibilities of
joint movement. Many joints allow rotation, and the combination
of bending, stretching and twisting enables us to screw, swerve,
twist and turn with fluent, pliable movement. Twisting and turning
are closely related and interdependent movements, but the terms are
not synonymous. Turning involves the whole body which moves,
rotating in space to face new directions, while twisting concerns
parts of the body which screw in opposite directions, making a
torsion between the moving parts. It is often the release of the
torsion which gives the initial impetus for turning, spinning and
whirling jumps or for directional changes. Considerable tension
builds up as the torsion increases, and when this is released the
natural reaction is for the body to spring resiliently back to a normal state and to use up the power which has been generated, by
turning or spinning. Conversely, twisting results if part of the body
stops turning, while the rest continues to do so.

The Photographs

The main purpose of presenting a visual image is to stimulate a sense of movement, but photographs can only show positions, brief moments caught by the camera, and they will only convey movement if the viewers will project themselves into the action, imagining the movement which could have led into and out of the position shown, and by trying to 'feel' the rhythm and phrasing of the action as a whole.

Flight expresses better than anything else the spirit and excitement of gymnastics, therefore the few photographs which are included have been selected to illustrate this aspect.

Photographer Don Holstead

Flight with stretching and widening

2
Flight with asymmetrical
stretching

3
Flight onto hands

4
Flight onto hands

5
Flight with arching

6
Flight with an asymmetrical stress

7
Flight with twisting onto hands

8
Off-balance flight

9
Flight assisted by rope

10   Partners flying on a rope

11, 12   Flight over apparatus with asymmetrical support

13, 14
Flight to arrive and balance on hands

Twisting and turning have many uses and add greatly to the manoeuvrability of the body and to flexibility in movement. Versatility is increased by the vastly greater range of movement which is opened up. More specifically, one learns to twist and wriggle out of many tricky situations such as loss of balance and heedless falls which can often be averted. As the importance of torsion and the power which can be generated through it is understood it can more readily be exploited for skills such as turning jumps, vaults and swings with turning, rotatory travelling and all directional changes. The games and athletics skills of throwing, kicking and hitting are also closely bound up with twisting and turning.

These movements stir the whole body, all parts are affected by twisting, and the trunk in particular, is livened up. Awareness of all parts of the body can be fostered because what is happening in various parts is clearly apparent. Attention can be focused on the parts which start the twist as well as on the parts which resist it. The latter are often parts which are bearing weight. The torsion in various parts of the body such as a shoulder, neck, spine or one hip arouse sensation of movement in these regions. All this experience and understanding contribute to greater kinaesthetic awareness and improved management of the body.

Twisting activates and strengthens all the oblique muscles of the body, numerous tiny muscles in the back and great sheets of muscle in the sides and front. The physical advantages of strength and resilience of the trunk can hardly be overestimated. The vital organs are contained within the trunk and they too are stirred and stimulated by vigorous movement. Twisting movements are also necessary to maintain normal mobility in the joints of the spine, shoulders and hips. Far too many people are unduly restricted in the hips. This joint seems to escape full use in ordinary daily living, and movement becomes limited. If people are to move freely and gracefully such restrictions should be corrected.

Development of twisting and turning

The process of twisting should be experienced, initially through experiments with quick, light, screwing movements and slower, stronger, sinuous twisting freely from side to side. A firm, broad base is needed to support the weight and give resistance to the twisting parts and a variety of weight bearing parts can form the base. Twisting combined with bending, stretching, rising and sinking, and moving through various planes, gives the feeling of pliant and flexible movement and overcomes the dullness and inflexibility of twisting back and forth in a horizontal plane. The effect of these trial twisting movements often leads to a loss of balance and inevitably, a transference of weight, or they lead to turning movements which spin the body, and such movements are the logical outcome of twisting. Having experienced twisting generally, investigations can then be made in how to transfer weight by twisting. Part of the body is fixed and supports the weight, while the free part twists and moves towards the floor in preparation for the weight to be transferred on to it. Continuous movement from one part of the body to another can be made in this way. Alternatively, vigorous twisting can initiate spinning and whirling through space. The resistant, fixed parts suddenly yield or are overcome, and the whole body rotates while travelling, or in turning leaps and jumps.

The limbs can be twisted inwards towards the midline of the body, or outwards away from it. The effect of twisting a limb should be felt; by rotating an arm or a leg the whole body can be turned and, unless resisted, the twisting spreads into the trunk and eventually turns it. Western Roll shows the effect on the body of twisting one leg. Investigation of these matters should be made from various starting positions, lying, kneeling, sitting, standing, hanging, and while moving. Sensible children can play a game of gently twisting a partner's arm or leg, both inwards and outwards, until the body turns over. Sequences of continuous movement can be made in this way.

The limits to which various movements can be taken should also be experienced. Holding a position at the limit will give a twisted shape to the body. Such shapes are necessary for versatility in action, particularly in jumping and balancing actions.

The kinaesthetic sensation of the dynamic changes should be felt. Tension grows and spreads through the body as the twisting is increased, and this is further intensified by the generation of inner resistance through one part of the body working against another. The release of the tension can range from being slow and controlled to sudden and explosive. The elasticity of the muscles can be clearly demonstrated through twisting movements. A sudden extra pressure at the limit of twisting can result in an explosive recoiling movement which initiates a flow of spinning movement along the ground or through the air. It is important that there should be no stop between the preparation of twisting one way and the recoiling executive movement the other way, for if there is a check, the power of the elastic recoil is lost. Spinning, preferably on a slippery surface, can be done from various starting positions such as sitting lightly or being poised on one knee or the ball of one foot. In the air the body can spin in various planes, in twirling leaps, and for those who have the skill and control, these movements are most exhilarating.

The ability to feel the sensation of twisting contrasted with turning, as well as the moment of changing from one to the other, gives added control of movement and more power to manage the body in action. The moments of change experienced as controllable and definable parts of actions, will be an aid in understanding and feeling the timing of more complex actions (page 120).

Lessons based on this material should include experience of many ways of twisting and turning in locomotion and flight as well as the more stable movements done on the spot. Inexperienced children can solve problems of twisting to transfer weight, including ways of turning over in rocking and rolling. They can twist through holes made by standing on all fours or in other starting positions, and work with partners to twist and turn, over, under and round one another. There is more certainty of ensuring that twisting really takes place if partners keep one or both hands joined while they move. Travelling on twisty pathways with many changes of direction and ever changing level, as well as simple jumps with twisting of the body or turning in the air, make a contrast to the more static movements without locomotion. Landings with turning, and the many ways of transferring weight with twisting and turning after landing, should also be practised. All the movements described in the section on bending and stretching can be done with twisting and turning, and should be experienced.

At an intermediate stage of skill, youngsters are generally interested in actions which test balance, and movements involving locomotion and flight. They may also enjoy an exploration of turning movements as opposed to twisting, and as a result of their experience become clearer about the difference and the relationship between the two. Problems of turning round various axes and moving in different planes can be given, but care must be taken to see that this does not become an academic exercise instead of an exploration and a mastery of movement.

Apparatus work must be included in the lessons and the material chosen should give ample opportunity for further development of the subject. New experience is opened up by being able to hang from arms, legs or body, and to twist or spin into and out of these situations. The range of heights, the size and inclination of surfaces, the variation in spaces offered by an interesting arrangement of apparatus, can give all the necessary stimuli.

The relationship of bending, stretching and twisting to gymnastic movement generally

That bending, stretching and twisting are an intrinsic part of gymnastic actions has been demonstrated repeatedly in the text. Frequent reference is made to the need to clarify the movements of the body, and the descriptions given in the two foregoing sections refer to the use of these body movements in gymnastic skills. A teacher with well trained powers of observation will recognise how and when bending, stretching or twisting occur in every type of action, in Transference of Weight, in Travelling, in Flight and in Actions emphasising Balance and also in apparatus work.

Bending, stretching and twisting being basic, are also an inclusive part of all other body movements. They are intrinsic in making Body Shapes and in Swinging and Circling. Symmetrical and asymmetrical movements as well as simultaneous and successive body movements are specialised ways of moving in which bending, stretching and twisting are done in specific ways. The sections on Bending and Stretching, and Twisting have been treated more fully than the other sections because of the vital role these movements play in all action. The body is the instrument of movement and in order to 'play' it well, it must be 'tuned' to a fine pitch.

Making body shapes

Body Shape refers to the form of the body when holding a position. Many references are made to body shape throughout the text, and the sections on Bending, Stretching, and Twisting, often mentioned position. These positions should be stressed when body shape is being considered for positions are Body Shapes. The relation of movement to the centre of the body, and the way of moving into and out of positions, are discussed in the previous sections, and these matters are also relevant in lessons on Body Shape.

Rounded shapes are formed by curling the body round the centre; this can be in any direction, curving backwards into an arched shape, or rounding over one side for forward. The rounding movement will come to a stop automatically when the physical limits are reached, but if movement is arrested before this, the body will, all the same, have a rounded shape, though more open and less compact than the shapes which come about through moving to the limits. Curved and rounded shapes are needed particularly for tumbling, rocking and rolling so that the weight can be transferred smoothly from one part to another.

Long narrow shapes are formed by reaching away from the centre in diametrically opposed directions. They have a feeling of penetrating into space and they occur in upspring jumps or vaults, or dives on to the hands, or for shooting, long and thin, into off-balance jumps. The body shape in many starting and finishing positions is the long and narrow one of poised, upright carriage.

Wide shapes are the result of extending and at the same time spreading the body. The two matching sides are drawn away from the midline to make the whole body form a broad, wide shape. Cartwheels, wide jumps, or actions such as scrambling along wall bars or window ladders with big steps, incorporate these shapes. In games one often makes oneself wide to act as a barrier to hinder an opponent from getting past, and to defend the territory behind.

Twisted shapes grow out of twisting movement. Twisting is generally combined with bending and stretching, and a variety of twisted shapes arise when these movements are arrested, e.g. a twisted round shape is often assumed for rolling, or a twisted arched shape may form the climax of a jump.

Actions sometimes depend on a shape which is *held* while the body as a whole moves; rocking and rolling actions, and cartwheels are typical. The climax of some actions is a clear body shape assumed slowly as in some balancing skills or swiftly as in jumps, and to 'arrive' and hold a clear shape is the object in many vaults and balances. The body shape *changes* constantly in all movement, and this is clearly seen in actions such as rope climbing, monkey travelling under bars or twisting in and out of window ladders.

It is important to stress that body shape comes about because of the movement leading up to it. Children who do not understand this often strike poses which bear no relation to what has happened or what will happen afterwards. This relation of movement to shape is very clearly seen by stopping a film of action. Movement is 'frozen' by the stop, and shows 'shape' at this moment, then is 'unfrozen' by the continuation; so 'shape' is movement momentarily 'caught' and held. Shapes and positions should be active and vital because of the tensions and counter-tensions in all parts of the body; these are held in balance so that visible movement ceases. An awareness of body shape helps to clarify both the purpose and the execution of actions, and clarity of movement and position are needed for precision in all spheres of skill.

Symmetric and asymmetric movement of the body

In spite of the natural symmetry of the body everyday movements are mainly asymmetric. Right handed people stress the right side, but to bring about harmonious movement, the non-stressed side makes compensatory movements to counterbalance the action of the stressed side. A right handed tennis player, javelin thrower or bowler uses the whole body because the left side makes active counterbalancing movements while the right side carries out the intended action. But the actions in some sports are symmetrical particularly in swimming where breast stroke, dolphin and certain dives depend on identical movement of the two sides of the body.

The movements of gymnastics can be:

> *Symmetrical* when both sides of the body move together doing exactly the same thing, e g a star jump or leap frog.

> *Asymmetrical* when one side of the body is stressed more than the other so that the two sides do not match, e g any twisting movement or jump with turning.

> *Alternate* when alternate sides are stressed. One side starts and the other side repeats the first movement identically as in crawling, walking or running.

The ideas can be developed in gymnastics lessons and movement becomes more accurate as awareness of the various ways of moving increases. Symmetrical movements can only occur in an up-down and forward-backward direction because any twisting, turning or sideways movement makes a one-sided stress and takes the body into asymmetrical action. It needs accuracy to make symmetrical jumps or vaults in which both feet take off together, both hands grasp apparatus simultaneously and the movements of both sides of the body are identical. To develop such bodily discipline experience should be given in ways of supporting and transferring weight on matching parts of the body. Rocking, rolling, weight transference, jumping and balancing skills can all be done symmetrically. Many of the traditional skills emerge through experimenting with symmetrical ways of moving, and skills such as headstand, handstand

and forward roll, dive rolls and handsprings frequently occur. In all such actions matching weight-bearing parts support the body, the movement of the two equal sides of the body are identical, and all held positions stress bodily symmetry. Symmetrical actions have a feeling of balance and control, therefore, they are easy to restrain and stop.

Asymmetrical movement can go into all directions and feels much freer. Many actions can give experience of moving and holding the body asymmetrically, for example, weight bearing on single or non-matching parts of the body, asymmetrical ways of transferring weight, travelling with swerving, twisting and turning, and jumps in which the two sides of the body do not match. These ideas are also used in apparatus work, for example, in spinning on ropes or rings while hanging by one leg or arm, or in vaulting when the weight is supported and the body is moved with a one-sided stress, or in turning jumps through bars or round poles and in the free leaps and bounds from boards or trampettes in which the body is moved and held asymmetrically. Asymmetrical body movement has a feeling of unbalance and easily leads to locomotion, and it is much more difficult to restrain and stop.

Alternate sided actions give a sense of balance because of the equalising effect of one side repeating the action of the other. Loco-motor actions such as skipping or springing with huge strides stress alternate sides equally, similar actions, moving on various parts of the body, are discovered when experimenting with this idea. On apparatus, alternate sided action can be made while travelling on bars (forward, backward, with rotation and monkey travelling), climbing up window ladders, or balancing, or jumping along forms or bars.

Actions are hardly ever purely one thing or the other but are a mixture of everything. Part of an action may have a particular stress such as the body shape at the climax of a jump, which can have symmetrical or asymmetrical form, and in balancing skills, the movements which lead to the final position may start symmetrically, and then change so that the last part and the final position are asymmetrical. Actions such as cartwheels show how a one-sided movement can lead to the symmetrical wheel shape of the body at the climax of the action.

Movement affects the state of equilibrium of the body while it is in the air. It is possible to be flying through the air while the two sides of the body move, or are held, in an identical way, in the way a swallow dive is made, or the way the body is moved and held in a dive or a symmetrical handspring. Here the body feels balanced and any twisting or leaning to one side would disturb balance and send the body into a rotation, and make it much more difficult to manage. Off-balance flying and falling always have an asymmetrical stress (page 64). The balanced gliding of a gull compared with the wild tumbling of a lapwing demonstrate perfectly, balance and symmetry, and asymmetry and off-balance, in flight.

Lessons based on this material are for people who have covered the basic background and who have had considerable experience of movement. They should have an understanding of bending, stretching, twisting, turning and making body shapes, and general actions such as weight bearing and body balance and various aspects of locomotion and flight. Every gymnastics lesson should aim to do something to build up an understanding and feeling for good carriage and the opportunities in lessons based on this material are outstanding. The symmetrical, balanced build and even development of the body should be the outcome of healthy growth, and we should do what we can to help people to develop a well poised body and gain the grace of balanced, harmonious carriage.

Simultaneous and successive movement of the body

'Simultaneous' and 'successive' here refer to the ways movement flows to and from, and through the body. It can travel through the body by means of a rippling type of movement which affects part after part successively or by movement in which all parts move together, simultaneously. The former resembles the wave-like movement which travels along a rope if one end is undulated, and the latter like the reaction of a compressed spring when it is released; every part of the spring moves simultaneously. Successive movement is started by an impulse and flows from part to part until the momentum dies down. This type of movement has a tendency to flow on, with a feeling of going beyond the body, or leading to further movement. Simultaneous movement, on the other hand is also started by an impulse but it affects all parts at once, and flows on to a finish. The chief importance of this in gymnastics is that people should be able to select the way of moving which is most appropriate for what they are doing. Both ways are part of gymnastics (and all other movement), but there is much less scope for exploiting successive movements than there is in dance. Body waves, successive movements, are important in gymnastics because they are effective and harmonious ways of adjusting the body weight.

Simultaneous movement is experienced in actions such as:

> Vaults like leap frog, squat vaults over apparatus and upsprings from apparatus.
>
> 'Arriving' on apparatus to stop.
>
> Jumps with immediate stopping on landing.
>
> Making Body Shapes.
>
> Moving into position in Balance Skills.

These actions, and many others like them, are based on the body movements of bending and stretching in which all parts move at the same time.

Successive movement is experienced in actions such as:

> Some wheeling actions on the floor and over apparatus.
>
> Body waves under bars, or with the help of partners, or between ropes, or at wall bars, or down from apparatus.
>
> Swinging on ropes or bars to arrive on apparatus with a body wave.
>
> Jumping on to bars to swing through and land far forward.
>
> Vaults through pommels of horses or over boxes, to land far forward.
>
> Weight transference started by twisting.
>
> Jumps started by twisting.

The actions listed above are based on the body movements of bending, stretching and twisting. Twisting is typically successive movement. The twist is initiated by one part and spreads to the next and successive parts until it is stopped by the resistance of the torsion, or released in turning movement.

Simultaneous movement is experienced and developed through bending and stretching. It is necessary to make all parts of the body take part, and see that no movable part is omitted from the movement. Some children find this difficult and move some parts of the body while other parts are held inactive. It is, for instance, common to see children curling up, but moving only the arms and upper part of the body, while the legs and hips are not incorporated in the action. Similarly, people often come down from inverted positions on to an inelastic stiff leg and then make a clumsy recovery to uprightness. The bending in the whole body (including the receiving leg) should continue until the whole weight is over the feet, when the stretching movement, which brings the body up, can begin.

All parts of the body do not necessarily move in like manner; some parts may move faster than others, and some parts may make more extensive movement, in which case asymmetrical action results.

Successive movement occurs in two types of body wave, one in which the weight is adjusted in the air before landing, and the other in which it is moved from one base to another after landing. Wave-like movements are made in the former, during the flight, to adjust the weight in actions such as heave swings (swings through bars), or through vaults (vaults between the arms) with a long forward thrust. At one point the body 'lies' in the air, nearly horizontal, and at the height of the flight it is brought to the vertical, ready for landing, by means of a wave of movement which starts by swinging the legs down, and continues by a rippling movement through all parts of the body successively to affect the head and arms last. These heave swings through bars are dangerous unless people are able to make this weight adjustment. Many have no trouble and do it naturally, but some swing forward, release the bar and fall on their backs, having made no adjustment to bring themselves to the vertical. When such bar swings are first introduced, they are safer, if at the height of the swing a strong twist is made to turn the body over so that the landing is made facing the bar. This is also a successive movement, the twist, initiated at the hip, travels up the body, part by part, to affect the arms and head last.

The other typical wave-like movement occurs when the landing creates a situation in which the body is momentarily 'slung' between two points as in hanging on a low bar with feet forward on the floor. This happens often in gymnastics, and the skilful reaction on landing is to adjust the weight over the second base, by means of a body wave. The movement is very often made awkwardly, so this is one of the skills which should be carefully taught. Body waves can be practised at wall bars which are stable and give an easy grip, but low bars or poles, two ropes or a partner can also be used. An exercise can be taken in which the starting position is sitting up straight on the floor or a form, with legs crooked, by the wall bar, the back close against the wall bar with the hands grasping it as high as possible. A wave is then made to lift and swing the body forward and up on to the feet. The movement always starts with a pull on the wall bar and a forward upward swing of the hips to take them high above the feet. As the hips move, the knees straighten and then the movement ripples up through the hips, spine, neck, head and arms. The head and arms lift last and accentuate the rise of the wave. The youngsters should first be allowed to try. When they have taken up the starting position, they can experiment with the task of changing the weight up on to the feet with a big wave-like movement. By observing the class the teacher will see what help is needed. Some need very little, but it is likely that nearly everyone will have to be coached to stretch the knees fully. This is necessary for giving a stable 'pillar', to hold the body up, while the wave rises through the body. The head moves last, therefore, it should be held back until the movement reaches the neck. The tendency is to lift the head too early – to thrust it forward – and this prevents any possibility of successive movement through the upper part of the spine. Instead, the upper part of the body moves awkwardly, all-in-a-piece. The strength of the initial impulse which sets the wave in motion, is important. If it is too light, it dies out before the wave reaches completion, and if it is too violent, it starts a rush of movement which is liable to upset balance.

Most youngsters enjoy practising body waves and as they are very effective in developing pliability and feeling for movement in the trunk; regular practice is to be encouraged. When the symmetrical waves, just described, have been mastered, variations should be tested. Grips and foot positions can be changed, other apparatus can be used and the wave can be made with twisting. Further experiments can be made to discover what can logically happen when the wave reaches the top and breaks.

Movement is never one thing or the other, in the way described, but generally a blending. A body wave starts with the lifting of the hips – simultaneous movement – which only becomes successive when the wave starts. Heave swings on bars start with simultaneous movement (both the jump and the swing forward of the whole body), and successive movement follows to adjust the weight. Jumps with twisting and turning start with successive movement, but turning, in which the body moves as a whole is simultaneous movement. Ability to feel and control the way movement flows through the body gives increased command of it. A high degree of awareness is needed to feel what all parts are doing, and the shape of movement becomes clearer through this.

Comparing the use of successive and simultaneous movement, and discovering how and when each is used can be used as a lesson theme for those who have had considerable movement experience and who understand what they are doing.

Swinging and circling

Swinging and circling are ways of moving the limbs or the whole body, to and fro, or round and round, about a fixed point. The fixed point may be part of the body, the arms can swing from side to side round the trunk, or one arm can circle from the shoulder. On the other hand, when the body swings or spins on ropes, or round bars, or over horses, the fixed point is outside the body.

Swinging and circling movements make use of outside forces, gravity or centrifugal force, acting upon the weight of the swinging part. In order to make this part weighty, it must become heavy and relaxed. A charge of energy from the centre of the body generally initiates each swing and augments the energy imparted by the external force. This makes problems in the management of the body for, though the swinging part must be heavy, the rest of the body must be full of vitality in order to keep control and give direction to movement.

Swinging has its own natural rhythm and gives a sensation which is much enjoyed by most people. The repetitive accents and the regularity of pendulum swings helps many unrhythmical people to feel a sense of rhythm. As well as feeling the rhythm while they are swinging, they can be helped further by watching and feeling inside themselves, the regular rhythm of a swinging climbing rope, a ring or a trapeze.

Some form of swinging or circling will probably be included in every lesson. Youngsters should be encouraged to swing and spin on ropes, rings, trapezes, bars and poles. They can hang by many different parts of the body, upside down as well as right way up. These are generally safe ways for children to get high into the air, to turn upside down and see the world from another viewpoint, and to spin and see things whizzing round them. These experiences, height, inversion and turning, are all common causes of fear, therefore, care must be taken with timid children to allow them to experiment in their own ways and time. There are many investigations to make with swinging. Children generally experiment with:

> Ways of supporting the body weight by twining ropes round various parts of the body.
>
> Ways of 'recharging' the swinging, with and without the use of the floor.
>
> Discovering ways of stopping the swing with control.
>
> Discovering the different speeds and size of swing when hanging under or standing up on rings or trapezes.

Finding the effect of changing shape, from wide to narrow and vice versa, while spinning on a ring.

Swinging the arms or legs can be the preparation which gives impetus for movement to the whole body. An arm swing often helps to propel the body in jumping, as in broad jumps. Leg swinging is used in many jumps and vaults; the swing augments the propulsion gained from the take-off and also gives direction to the movement. The whole body swings in order to carry it onwards in hand traveling on bars. Twisting the trunk combined with swinging the arms or legs or both, gives impetus for spinning actions and whirling jumps. When swinging is used in preparation for an action, it should work up by starting gently, with small movements which get bigger and faster until the last swing, in which the impetus for the action is released. A common fault is to make all the swinging movements of equal size and power. This destroys any feeling for the timing and the building up to the climax, which is such an important aspect of rhythm in action.

Swinging and circling are economical ways of gaining momentum for movement, but considerable movement skill and understanding are necessary before swinging and circling movement can be used with full effect. Therefore, lessons based wholly on this material are more suitable for experienced people. There are interesting problems, both for teacher and class, in the exploration and full exploitation of this material.

Movement emphasising special parts of the body

i. The parts of the body which initiate, guide or counteract movement

The impetus for movement is always *initiated* by some specific part of the body. Bending, stretching and twisting are initiated and controlled mainly by the trunk, but the limbs can also start movement, particularly to give impetus for spinning and turning.

The task of *guiding* movement through space is always done by definite parts of the body. Any part which is about to receive the weight guides the whole body to the place of arrival. This part must move appropriately, with well judged speed and direction, ready to receive the weight with control. In landing, generally the toes guide the movement to the place of arrival, and to stand on the head, to kneel or to sit, the body is guided into position by the parts which will receive the weight. To hang or arrive on apparatus, the hands, legs or other parts reach out, ready to take the weight, guiding the body to the point of arrival.

Movement is guided through space for other purposes. The chest is the natural part for guiding the body in rising movements. It is the lightest and most buoyant part and, therefore, most appropriate for this task. The sternum generally guides movement high into the air in jumping, but it is possible for other parts of the chest to do the same, and many lively leaps and jumps come about by stressing one side or part of the back. The hips and pelvis, firm, strong parts of the body, guide movement when the body is lowered. If equilibrium is to be maintained the hips must be guided so that the centre of gravity falls vertically over the supporting base, but if weight is to be transferred they must guide to unbalance the body in the desired direction. Turning movements, and all directional changes, can be guided by various parts of the trunk or limbs, and the head can also lead movement into any direction. In the course of action new impulses are initated for every change, and the guidance of movement passes from part to part in the twisting, whirling, rising, falling, rushing and sudden stopping.

To keep control of the body, some parts move to *counteract* the main action. For instance, in such everyday actions as going downstairs or stepping off a chair, or gymnastic actions such as sliding head or feet first off horses or boxes, gravity pulls downward and this is counteracted by an upward pull through the body to control the downward speed. Similarly in skills such as handstand followed by rolling on the back or the front, or backward somersault from a bar, the main direction of motion is counteracted by a strong pull in the opposite direction by the hips and legs. This controls the speed, but if no resistance is made, then everything goes in the same direction and control is greatly diminished. It is a common fault in all examples cited to allow gravity to 'dictate'. This is often caused by lack of understanding and poor kinaesthetic sense, and can generally be corrected by advice to hold back with the legs.

To move in a balanced way, in alternate sided forms of locomotion such as walking or skipping, the actions of the legs and lower trunk are counterbalanced by rotation of the upper trunk and the alternate arm swing. Similarly, in games and athletics, the skills which have a one-sided stress such as hurdling, throwing or tennis strokes, all need movements to counteract, balance and control the stressed parts of the actions. Hurdlers pay much attention to the leading arm which counteracts the stressed movement of the leading leg, and in right-handed hitting or throwing, active resistance in the left side of the body, counteracts the body rotation, the weight transference, and the arm movement, and keeps the action, as a whole, in control.

ii. *The legs, trunk and arms*

The children may reach a point of skill when the teacher sees the need to concentrate exclusively on the use of particular parts of the body for two or three lessons. Such lessons will generally take the form of revision in which previous experience is tested and used in new ways. The knowledge of the ways in which parts of the body can be used is pinpointed and summarised.

The legs

The legs are the chief weight bearers and they carry the body in all forms of locomotion and flight. Good leg work can influence the general quality of movement and when they are moved in a vital and skilful way this has an all round enlivening effect on the body. The dull, slovenly and limited way in which many people habitually use their legs has a deadening effect on their movement. Therefore, in lessons on Leg Awareness progress is made through experiencing the great variety of work done by the legs and by feeling how quality of movement made by them carries over to movement of the body generally.

The main uses of the legs are:
To support the weight on the ground or suspended on apparatus, and through gripping, in such actions as rope climbing or monkey travelling.

To carry, propel, project and receive the weight in locomotion and flight.

To lower and raise the body while moving and changing position.

To initiate movement and give impetus for actions such as twisting and turning jumps, and spinning movements.

To add momentum for swinging and circling movements.

To guide movement through space for 'arriving', or for directional changes.

To provide counteraction in many skills.

To control balance particularly in inverted positions.

The spine, trunk and head

Use of the spine, trunk and head are vital for harmonious, flowing movement. The trunk unites the whole body in movement by acting with both lower and upper limbs. The structure of the spine (with compressible discs between the bodies of the vertebrae and numerous tiny movable joints between adjoining vertebrae) allows extensive pliable movement through a combination of twisting, bending and stretching. The movements are initiated and controlled by the trunk; movement flows to and from it or peripherally round the centre. The intricate musculature of the spine and trunk gives it flexibility with strength and resilience, provided it is put to constant and vigorous use. The concentration of strong muscular tension around the lower trunk, hips and legs gives the power and firmness needed for strong movements. Strength and firmness are imperative for lifting, carrying, pushing, pulling or supporting heavy objects and for tussling with, or handling partners. The whole trunk, back, sides and abdomen are also firmly held in these actions, but with flexible, resilient strength and with readiness to adapt and adjust according to need. Emphasis shifts to the upper part of the trunk, chest and arms when lightness and buoyancy of movement are required, and there is much less tension. The chest is the centre of light movement and the pelvis the centre of strong movement.

The neck and head move with the spine, twisting, circling and arching to carry through to completion movements started in the trunk. But because equilibrium is disturbed by movements of the head, many unskilled people make awkward and restricted movements in an endeavour to keep the head upright or still. People should be taught how to incorporate their heads in their movements, and be given plenty of experience in doing it. As they become more skilful and feel how the head should move, there will be a marked effect in freeing and harmonising movement. The head sometimes leads movement; it moves to allow the eyes to follow the direction which the movement takes.

The poise and carriage of the body are affected by the way the trunk and head are balanced and held. The upright, poised carriage of the human being depends on an intricate combination of body-mind factors, therefore physical efforts on their own can only play a part in developing a poised and graceful carriage. Teachers can, however, help their pupils to feel how to hold themselves poised, with the body lifted and a light grip around the centre to brace the body and prevent heaviness and sagging. A poised stance is the starting position for a great many actions; and an upright and easy carriage terminates many actions, and in addition, poised carriage of the body is an integral part of good movement generally.

It is all too easy to neglect the movements of the trunk in gymnastics lessons. People can leap and jump, balance, swing and do many things without much feeling for movement or understanding of what they are doing. For skilled management more is needed, and an important matter is an underlying feeling for what the body itself is doing, how and when it flexes, extends or twists, and how these movements are blended harmoniously and rhythmically to give truly expert execution of actions. Through increased kinaesthetic awareness, the body becomes more finely co-ordinated, capable of more skilled and sensitive use.

Lessons can be based on movement of the trunk and spine, but these should be for people who have progressed beyond the elementary stage and who are interested in gaining greater mastery of themselves. The spine and trunk are used in all actions, therefore, the choice and variety of material which can be used for illustration of the principles are unlimited. Lessons stressing the use of the spine and trunk are a way of revising themes which have emphassised other aspects of movement. The progressive stages naturally depend on work already covered, and might work out:

Classes with least experience could concentrate on the trunk work in actions which clearly stress bending, stretching and twisting.

The next stage could revise actions which incorporate body shapes, including symmetrical and asymmetrical actions, and investigate the role played by the spine and trunk in this.

A yet more advanced stage could clarify the bodily aspects of actions involving balance or flight or both combined, including the use of successive and simultaneous movement.

The arms

The most natural use of the arms is to co-ordinate with the movements of the upper trunk and head, and these depend on the movements of the rest of the body. In daily life the arms are the most used and most co-ordinate part of the body, the most kinaesthetically developed and obedient members, and this aptitude can be utilised for all movement teaching. One can often 'teach' other parts of the body through the arms. Small movements of the feet and actions of the legs can quickly become livelier and more co-ordinated if accompanied by similar movements of the hands and arms. Arm movements can also give the feeling of various qualities of movement, which having been consciously experienced in this situation, are more easily transferred to the feeling of movement in the body generally, e g the hands and arms are generally responsive in making sudden or light movement, where this might be more difficult to feel in the whole body, but at least one step is taken through understanding what is required.

The function of the arms and shoulders in actions such as walking, running, hopping and jumping is often neglected and people let their arms flop about, and flay around, in an uncontrolled manner. The function in skilled actions is often to supplement and counterbalance movement, and it is worthwhile discovering how to carry and move the arms in order to get full control in action. The arms are used in many of the same ways as the legs for gymnastics, and they are able to:

> Support weight with the body inverted, and grip in various ways to hang and climb.

> Push, pull, lift, carry, support or grasp, partners or objects.

> Receive and carry the weight in locomotion and flight.

> Initiate, give impetus and add momentum to movement.

> Guide movement through space to arrive, or for directional changes.

> Provide counteraction and counterbalance in many actions.

Body Themes related to gymnastics

Each of the ideas described in this section can be developed as themes for lessons (page 141). The Body Themes can also be combined with Action, Movement or Space themes which give lessons a double stress such as:

> Bending and Stretching with Weight Transference (Action).
> Symmetry and Asymmetry with On- and Off-balance (Action).
> Twisting and Turning with variations of Speed (Movement).
> Simultaneous and Successive movement with Continuity and Stopping (Movement).
> Making Body Shapes and using the Personal Space (Space).
> Turning in various planes and through all Levels (Space).

DYNAMIC ASPECTS OF ACTION

Movement quality and effort

The dynamic aspects of action are to do with the way we use our movement powers. The physiological and psychological processes which trigger off these powers are exceedingly complex and, therefore, obviously cannot be dealt with here. The physiologists and the psychologists as well as Rudolf Laban's writings and the various Art of Movement Centres will give more information. We know that movement takes time, uses energy and needs space (Time, Weight and Space Factors of Motion). It is the way the individual blends these components which gives all the shades of quality to movement. The shades of quality depend on the way people, voluntarily or involuntarily, control all the factors which bring about changes of muscular tension, for ultimately it is muscles which enable us to move. But movement is also affected by the way we think and feel, by our attitude to what we are doing, as this influences the way we set about carrying out our intentions.

Rudolf Laban used the term Effort to describe this body-mind interdependence in the control of movement and he devised a form of Effort training to give people greater command of themselves. Effort training is given as part of movement education in dance teaching, and a modified form of it is also used in teaching objective skills. The purpose is to develop awareness and mastery of the dynamic aspects of action for it is this which makes movement effective and gives it quality. The great range of effort qualities which are possible in the free, unhampered movement of dance, are not equally possible in objective movement, for practical tasks are subject to external conditions which determine, to a point, how things must be done. To serve in tennis, the ball must be hit with a given amount of power and speed to get it over the net and into court. Similarly, to pull the body up to a bar requires that enough power is exerted to overcome the resistance of the weight. Observation will, however, show that there is great variation in the way these things are done, so in spite of laid down conditions people have considerable freedom to choose their own ways. There is no one absolutely right way to kick, hit, throw, leap, run or move, and we have discovered that what is right for one person is not necessarily best for another. Teachers must try to detect every child's natural way of moving, and thereby be able to help each one according to the most effective way for the individual. But because there are set conditions, people must be helped to recognise them and learn to master their movement powers so that they can do whatever they wish, to the limits of their ability.

Control of energy and tension

The effort training which is given through gymnastics is concerned with energy control which affects the way changes in muscular tension are made (gradually, suddenly, explosively, lightly, resiliently) to give effective movement. All these changes can be felt kinaesthetically, and we can learn how it feels to impart force to the body (or parts of it) to move it, how to get a grip to hold the energy in the body, how to use the resiliency of the body, and generally feel and become aware of how energy output is controlled. This training is done, as far as possible, through the functional actions of gymnastics, but there are times when the teacher will see the need to give more direct help with the dynamic content of an action. Some people have so little command of themselves that they cannot feel how to use their powers and they need help and experience in how to do so. When this lack is apparent, the teacher can devise exercises, based on the dynamic changes which occur in the actions, and through these give experience which will help to improve the efficiency and quality of performance. The principle is for the teacher to discover the most important and accented moments in an action, and the parts where the speed and tension changes are most marked, and then invent a simple practice in which similar dynamic changes can be experienced in a consecutive and rhythmic sequence of movement. Such exercises also help to pinpoint the timing, clarify the rhythm and induce a flow of movement, and these are matters which are of great importance if action is to be skilful, economical and harmonious. A few examples of such exercises are given in the text (pages 60 and 77) and in this section two examples are given on page 114. The descriptions of the Actions of Gymnastics repeatedly refer to dynamic aspects through the use of words such as strong, powerful, shoot, compress, bouncy, explosive, suddenly, gradually, lightly, and all convey quality, how to move.

Development of dynamic aspects of action

Gymnastics reveals a number of common factors in movement such as ways of yielding to gravity and overcoming it, different ways of moving and checking movement and combinations of these. Further general considerations are how contact is made and how things are touched (with various parts of the body), as well as how partners or apparatus are handled. Ways of twisting, bending and stretching are likewise common factors in action, and all these general movements will be used as examples to illustrate how, through gymnastics, experience can be given and understanding be developed of the dynamic aspects of action.

The general principles underlying all movement are briefly described in Part I (page 11). Examples of how these principles are used in practice are given in this section. The Flow and Space Factors of Motion are dealt with in a general way in relation to gymnastics, and the Time and Weight Factors are illustrated through the specific movements listed below:

Yielding to gravity and overcoming it.

Moving and stopping.

Imparting energy and checking movement.

Body movements.

Touch and contact.

Handling.

The Time and Weight factors

Yielding to gravity and resisting it

This occurs in many actions, whenever one sinks towards the ground or rises up away from it and it is, therefore, important to learn what it really feels like to yield, and in contrast to fight and overcome gravity and resist it. The first point to feel and apprehend is the effect of gravity on the body weight. Gravity draws us towards the ground and our ability to resist the pull, lifts and holds us up, away from the ground. People should experience the feeling of yielding, letting go, in different ways, gradually or fast, and using their 'braking' power, when tension is suddenly released, to stop the downward rush of the body. Yielding and sinking right to the ground, to finish lying quite relaxed on the floor, should be stressed in the initial stages of learning. Feeling various ways of getting off the ground must also be experienced and this can be done swiftly and forcefully enough to shoot the body into the air, or more slowly, in a gentler way, 'growing' away from the ground until high above it, and moving away with lightness. The amount of tension needed for light movement is just enough to counteract the effect of gravity. If there is too little, movement becomes slack, without quality and heavy and if there is too great tension, movement is often restricted and ungainly.

Yielding first and recovering after, as two separate processes, are only the beginning of learning which helps people to recognise and be able to control the different sensations of yielding to gravity and resisting it. In harmonious, economical action, there is always an interplay, yielding leads resiliently into recovery as the body sinks and rises. For this the natural elasticity of the body comes into play and it is important that people should learn to use the recoiling powers of their muscles since much energy is saved by exploiting this aptitude. It is a gift which everyone has, in greater or lesser degree, some people are naturally resilient while others may be over-slack or too tense, but resilience is a power which can be developed. To be able to use ones resilience depends to a considerable extent on attitude of mind; those with the will, can go a long way to feeling buoyant and resilient, and they are then better able to sense and produce the rhythmic alternation of the stronger and lighter efforts which give resilient changes in movement. Control of the dynamic changes which occur in rising and sinking are needed for a great many gymnastic actions. Examples can be found in 'Transference of weight' (pages 26f, 29), in 'Flight' (pages 41 and 45), and 'Balance actions' page 60) in which the need is stressed for control of speed and tension in the rhythmic changes of resilient movement.

Moving and stopping

This is a fundamental concept of movement and one easily grasped by beginners. The elements of the Time Factor – suddenness and sustainment – can be experienced through lightning quick movement which gives a sensation of suddenness, and much slower movement which gives a sensation of lingering and prolonging the duration of time. Quickness is needed for sudden starting, stopping, turning, grasping, taking-off, and sudden bending, stretching or twisting, and all these movements are part of the actions of gymnastics. Slow movement is used for careful lowering of the body or placing parts of the body on apparatus, or for controlled weight changes, and for gradual stopping, starting, turning and all slow body movements. Beginners benefit by experiencing the extremes. Everyone has a different tempo and what is quick for one may be quite slow for another, and it is a help to see this. It may also be helpful to establish some absolute between teacher and class so that words such as sudden, swift, quick, slow, sustained or lingering, come to have more specific meaning. Observation also helps a class to come to an understanding, and this can be done by comparing the efforts of various people in the class. Observation must, however, always be followed by putting into action what has just been learnt since it is only by the experience of actually doing that any real understanding can develop. It is also useful for the teacher to have a good stock of words and images to clarify the ideas and to stimulate the children while they are experiencing the qualities which their actions evoke. Moving through space at different speeds should also be experienced and this can be given through all forms of locomotion (page 33) and jumping. These actions can be made at a uniformly swift or slow speed and it may be a worthwhile experience to try to do this, but in natural movement the speed in action always fluctuates, and people should be helped to find the speeds which are appropriate to what they are doing. It is easier to concentrate and gives better practice if the actions are broken up into short phrases, short dashes with pauses, or a few slow steps (on feet or other parts of the body) and a pause. Playing with acceleration and deceleration (and the reverse) gives control and should be practised. Starting or stopping can be done gradually or suddenly. All races start suddenly and quickness has to be maintained, to the end, and many games skills need quickness off the mark, followed often by sudden stopping, to trick an opponent. Vaulting and jumping, and skills in which bodily balance and direction are important, often start slowly, and gradually accelerate to the moment of execution which is the sudden explosive movement which precedes the climax, often a much slower part of the action. Acceleration gives momentum which is needed particularly for leaping and vaulting, and it also adds velocity to objects thrown or struck. The ability to stop suddenly is also necessary for the avoidance of collisions, to check movement on 'arrival', and in some landings, and it is essential for skill and manoeuverability in games. A gradual deceleration is a natural way for speed to die down, and in fast actions, it is often by deceleration that the body is brought into control. To be able to move about, whirling, spinning with partners, dashing, checking and slowing up with good control, gives skill and confidence and is also a safety measure.

Imparting energy and checking movement

Movement is ultimately brought about by discharges of energy which activate our muscles, but in order to move, we do not have to know or even think about how the muscles act for they will work for us 'automatically'. But, to move well, we must be clear about what we want to do and how we wish to carry out our intentions and this depends on the skill and precision we have developed and the obedience of our bodies. We can learn to discharge energy with various intensities into the body and into selected parts; it is the control of this which gives the fine gradations, the sensitivity, power and quality which we see in the highly skilled.

Through sudden starting, stopping, grasping and other actions described in 'Moving and Stopping' people gain experience and learn how to impart impetus to the body to propel it, and how to get a grip to check movement for purposes such as changing direction or holding it motionless. To make a pause in movement, the body is gripped and held, with a lighter or a firmer tension, according to need. Firmness and stronger resistance must be exerted to check fast movement, and less power is needed to arrest slow movement. The different feeling of starting slowly or suddenly should be compared, and the lighter tension and less exertion which is needed for a gradual start can be contrasted with the sensation of preparing for and starting a race. In this there is an intense state of readiness, the body is full of stored power, ready to be released explosively, to propel the body fast on the starting signal.

Experience in a variety of dynamic changes can be given through a game-like play with movement, and the principles of moving and stopping suddenly, which is the basis of the children's game of 'Statues', will serve as an example of the use to which such ideas can be put. Movements such as running, scurrying on all fours, spinning, alone or with a partner, can all start the action. At the height of speed, the movement is suddenly stopped and held. The motion is counteracted by the resistance of the weight bearing parts gripping the floor, and the whole body is held firmly to keep every part still. People cannot always feel if they are quite still, so this can be tested by a self-examination, possibly prompted by questions from the teacher: Are you gripping the floor strongly? Is your body firm? Your hips? Legs? Is the whole of you still? This may help to induce bodily stillness. In the same sequence, further experience of effort changes occur if the firm, still position is gradually released and the body yields slowly, as if melting, until all tension has ebbed away and the body lies relaxed on the floor. Then there must be a short pause for recovery and preparation for whatever is to follow. As a complete contrast, the movement could be restarted by a swift gathering of the body through a strong contraction and a resilient change to shoot into the air before dashing off again through space.

Impulses of energy can be directed to any given part of the body to move them, and this happens when a part is selected for a particular role in movement. Always some specific part starts movement, other parts guide or control it and thus a series of body parts carry particular stress at various points in an action (page 101). A slashing leg can start a turning jump, or various parts of the thorax may guide the body upwards in rising movement; many examples are given throughout the text of the work done by specific parts of the body, and it is through the ability to stimulate these parts and direct the energy exactly where it is needed, that greater control of movement is achieved. Through careful observation, teachers will be able to see, at any specific moment, which part of the body should be animated, how people try to control their powers and whether or not they are directing their efforts in the best way and to the part of the body which is most important. Body awareness, as well as skill in the right selection and use of energy for action, are developed by attention being pinpointed to both the part of the body and the way of moving it.

Energy is discharged in various ways according to the purpose of actions. Jumps and other propulsive movements are started by an explosive release of energy which sets the body in motion, flinging it up into the air or propelling it along the ground. Body waves and other successive movements are started in the same way, sometimes more gently with the initial impulse giving impetus to the movement which travels through the body from part to part successively (page 96). A stress at the beginning starts movement which will continue until the momentum dies down or a new impetus is given. To stop movement suddenly makes a terminal stress which gives a feeling of finality and ending. The resistance of the weight bearing parts and the dynamic holding of all parts of the body, both arrest motion, as described above. Some simultaneous movement has a feeling of stopping and ending which is clearly sensed in a sudden arrival on apparatus or in landing with instant stopping. Energy is imparted in the middle of the action to keep a swinging motion going, and it is continually re-charged at a point between the beginning and end of the swing.

Body movements

Movements of the body itself are an intrinsic part of the actions of gymnastics, therefore, the speed and strength with which the body is bent, stretched or twisted has to be assessed and adjusted for effective and economical movement. Great speed is needed to bend and stretch the body to whip between the pommels of a saddle or through the narrow spaces between double bars, and swift strong extensions are part of such actions as upspring jumps. Balancing skills, on the other hand, often gain by being done more slowly and calmly, and a firm grip of the body, slowly released, will give more control in lowering the body from somersaults on ropes or bars, or from inverted positions. A quick, light twist can give a change of direction, and twisting is often needed for last moment adjustments of balance, or for turning the body over, as in rocking with turning, or in a continuous rope swing in which the hips and legs initiate a strong, sudden twist to turn the body over. Slower twisting gives more control when part of the body is getting ready to receive the weight, and sometimes a slow twisting movement generates power in preparation for a sudden, resilient release, to give impetus for spinning or turning. The 'moment of change' from bending to stretching (page 87), or twisting to turning (page 91), is the exact moment when new happenings start, when a release of tension begins or when energy is imparted to start movement. *When* things happen is a vital aspect of timing in action (page 120).

Two examples of effort training in relation to specific actions

Two examples of specific actions will suffice to show a way in which the dynamic content of an action can be 'extracted' and presented in simpler form for the purpose of experiencing kinaesthetically the type of dynamic changes which occur in each action.

In springing to snatch the whole body up close to a bar and to hold the tucked up position before slowly lowering and dropping lightly off, the outstanding events are: the contraction, the held position, the gradual release and the dropping off. These events can be simulated in a floor exercise. The starting position can be any lightly stretched position, with readiness to move. The first movement is a very powerful, swift gathering of the body which is then held in a firm contraction with all parts of the body gripping. The arms and shoulders should be held firmly against the body and the legs gripped tightly against the abdomen (as on the bar). A gradual release of this grip follows and the body is slowly and lightly stretched into a new starting position, ready for a repetition. Awareness of the moment of making each contraction and starting the release, gives control of the timing of the action. Such practices are only useful if the youngsters understand that they are learning by feeling how to make tension and speed changes, and that these effort changes are needed to help them at the bar. The practices should be quite short and they must be followed immediately by the action for which they were designed. It is clear that muscularly and in other ways the events on the floor are not exactly the same as those on the bar, but through such practices people learn to manipulate their muscular powers, and so become more conscious of them and more able to manage them.

Another typical gymnastic action is leaping and landing. The dynamic changes in this are so fast, especially those of the landing and recovery, that many people are unable to cope well with them. More control can be gained if experience is given in making the dynamic changes in a more manageable form. The feeling of the powerful thrust into the air, the change to flying lightly through it, the yielding right to the ground in the landing, can be simulated in a similar way to the last example, without actually jumping. The difficult parts of the sequence are changing the strong thrust of the jump into a lighter suspension in the flight, and then choosing the moment to yield. The effort exercise starts with the body in a slightly flexed, gathered position, with power held, ready to thrust. The first movement is a powerful upward thrust away from the ground, through the body, but without jumping. The jump is represented by this thrust. Elevation is emphasised by lifting the chest and head and can be further stressed by shooting one arm up. The sense of elevation is maintained (this represents the flight) while tension is released so that the body is held high up and moved lightly. The lightness is accentuated by easy breathing and by moving lightly away from the spot. The sensation of suspension is held longer than would be possible in a jump, and long enough to experience the feeling of being lightly held and high up in the air. At the right moment, the tension is released and the body yields softly to the floor. 'The right moment' depends on the rhythm of the whole. The exercise should become a rhythmic entity which feels pleasant. The whole time span, in such a practice, can be much longer than in a jump, and, therefore, there is time to experience the changes in different phases of the action. It will naturally be quite different doing it at the speed of a jump, but through such an exercise greater understanding can be gained of how to manage all the speed and energy changes in the various parts of a jump.

Similar practices should be devised by the teacher and incorporated in lessons at any time, as the need for them becomes apparent. Gymnastics is important as a means through which people can be taught to gain command of their powers.

Touch and contact

It is easy to become conscious of the pressure on any weight bearing part, and this simple way of increasing awareness can be experienced through practices in which the weight is held or moved over the many different parts of the body (pages 23 and 58). To be in full command of movement one should be able to control the way these parts touch or make contact with the supporting areas, for this skill is necessary for landing safely, for transference of weight, for grasping and releasing things and for balance skills. The different pressure sensations of a light touch, firmer pressure and weight bearing should be experienced, and touching the floor with various parts of the body should be tried. The hands, being the most sensitive and obedient members, can most easily feel the different qualities of touch and can, therefore, be used in 'teaching' the feet and other parts of both upper and lower limbs as well as the body itself. With the help of a partner (counterbalancing), many unusual parts of the body can be lowered to touch the ground lightly and lift away again, or, contact lightly and gradually take the weight. These experiments should be made from various starting positions, and with touching close to the body or far away. Such practices may at first be more effective if they are led and directed by the teacher, but as the youngsters gain experience and understand the purpose, they can be left free again to experiment without so much guidance.

It is a test of control to come down from low apparatus and first contact the ground lightly (with various parts) and only gradually increase the pressure, before releasing the apparatus and transferring the weight. It is good practice for uncontrolled children to try to resist the pull of gravity and lower themselves slowly from somersaults on bars, or reverse hanging on ropes or wall bars, to contact the floor lightly, before allowing the pressure on their feet to increase gradually, eventually to take their whole weight. When they gain enough control, they can try to come down and make the first light contact with other parts of the body such as the shins, seat, or one hip, before taking the whole weight on the part. As in all landings, the whole body must yield with great control while the weight is being received, and recover poise when the weight is safely on the supporting part. These skilful ways of arriving do much to foster awareness and control and they are a preparation for landings in more difficult forms of flight. Because the weight is supported the action can be slower, and this gives time for feeling how the receiving part prepares and also how the yielding starts at the moment of contact. Sometimes contact is made in quite another way, firmly and quickly, as it is when stopping instantly after fast movement or after a jump (page 48). Firm contact is also made when jumping to grasp apparatus to hang or arrive on it in other ways.

Transitory touch is stressed in some actions as in moving from part to part in light running landings or other forms of weight transference, as well as in the light touch of a hand, foot or other part, when flying over apparatus. If the weight is adjusted so that it can be moved instantly from part to part as each part touches, and is gradually slowed down, then nothing is jarred or bruised by undue pressure. Landings from swinging on ropes can provide opportunities for developing skill in light and transitory touch on landing. Children become absorbed by trying to finish swinging by touching down lightly and running on, partially supported by the rope, until they have control, when they let go and run on. They must judge, while they swing, when and where to touch the floor and when to let the rope go. It is exciting to work up a big swing and come down from a great height to judge the landing exactly right.

The way contact is made, maintained and released is important in many other actions; it matters how one helps, supports or releases a partner, or how one touches, grasps, holds and releases apparatus in climbing, hanging and vaulting. On the whole youngsters are not often aware of the way they come down, grasp, touch or hold things, and they will gain more control and feel surer when they realise that these things are within their control and that judgment is needed and will influence every situation. The quality of movement when contact is made depends not only on the part which touches but on the quality in the whole body. This in turn is controlled, consciously or subconsciously, by the individual. There must be the will to touch lightly or to grasp firmly and this affects the body as a whole. Concentration on the quality of touch or contact is another way of inducing the sensations associated with various degrees of strength and lightness.

Handling

The term Handling is used to describe actions in which external objects are manipulated. Energy can be transmitted to objects outside the body by pushing, pulling, lifting and supporting them. The amount of power exerted and the way it is used will depend on the weight of the object and the effect desired. How power is used is important in handling apparatus or partners as well as in all the tasks of lifting, and carrying, pushing and pulling which are part of everyday living. The principles which govern the way these tasks are done are common to all of them, therefore, it is valuable for school children to learn to understand them and be given enough practical experience.

Handling can be regarded as a form of weight lifting in which the weight and dynamic power of the body are pitted against heavy objects. In addition to having the utilitarian purpose of transporting apparatus, it can also be done in a much more lively and interesting way in the form of Partner and Group Work. The essence of Handling is the dynamic aspect of it, therefore, mention of it cannot be omitted from the part of the book which specifically deals with the dynamic aspects of action, but as fuller descriptions of the essential points have already been given in Part II in the sections entitled Handling (page 69) and Partner and Group Work (page 74), it is unnecessary to give more than this brief description here.

The Flow factor

The word flow in relation to gymnastics will be used to describe the synthesizing factor of movement, the factor which gives unity to separate parts, and wholeness, fluency and rhythm in action.

A flow of movement through space is started by unbalancing and propelling the body so that it travels through space, and it is checked by regaining body balance. Flow of another kind, through the body, can happen without travelling, and it comes about by bending, stretching and twisting the body. Movement through the body flows in towards and out away from the body centre, or round, or across the Personal Space surrounding the body (page 126). Movement can flow through the body either in a simultaneous or a successive way. Simultaneous movement affects all parts of the body at the same time, they start, go and finish simultaneously; the body stretching in upspring jumps and vaults, and the bending and stretching needed for rolling and springing up, demonstrate this. Movement is successive when first one part starts followed by the part adjoining, and so travels from part to part until the movement reaches completion; a body wave is a typical example of movement which is successive (page 98). Teachers must be able to observe both kinds of movement, how movement is started, recharged and stopped and how the body itself moves both while it is stationary or travelling. Flow and continuity in action depend on ability to phrase movement and knowing how to link phrases, and also on the right timing and rhythm of action.

Phrasing of movement and linking of phrases

Simple phrases have three parts, a preparation, a climax and a recovery, and movement must be phrased if it is to be effective and feel right. Every phrase has a starting point which leads naturally into the preparation. The preparation ends with a release of energy to bring about the climax which makes the point of the action and this is followed by the recovery. The discharge of energy makes an accent and this, together with the building up and dying down of tension gives rhythm to action. The rhythms of various types of action depend upon where in the phrase the main stress comes (page 113).

The structure of action patterns is analagous with the sentence structure of language. Words are put together to form phrases, and one or more phrases form a sentence. The linking of words and phrases, and the placing of stress and pauses gives the sentence meaning, rhythm and flow. Similarly, phrases of movement may be joined together to form sentences. The repetition of a simple phrase such as a few steps and a leap will give a repetitive, pulsating rhythm formed by the recurrent accent of the take-off. The whole sentence takes shape if there are a given number of repetitions, but if each is exactly the same, the sentence becomes monotonous, so the repetitions should vary slightly and might build up by starting with small light jumps and working up to a climax of one or more high, powerful leaps. Actions such as several successive jumps over the same horse, or repetitive leaps through bars or through a series of saddles, can be rhythmically developed in this way. Such skills demand anticipation and a readiness to recover from one action to go straight into the next. Generally the recovery phase of one action blends with the preparation for the next so that movement continues in a resilient, fluent way.

More intricate action patterns arise by linking unlike phrases to form movement sentences. These can be floor sequences such as a fluent combination of: taking weight over the hands, rocking on the back, springing up and getting ready to repeat, or, apparatus sequences such as: swinging round the upright of a bar, jumping over, and getting under the bar. This type of sequence is much more complex. The performer must get a clear picture of the whole and be able to anticipate how to lead fluently from one phrase into the next, and this depends on the *linking movements* in which the re-covery phase after the first climax is merged with the preparatory movements for the next phrase. This join may be simple and direct, or composed of several movements. The first sequence could be joined with simple links, the yielding landing after the weight comes down from the hands is linked, through sitting and rocking back and forward again to swinging up on to the feet, ready to repeat. The apparatus sequence is more complex. The four parts to be linked are the swing round the upright, the jump over, the move-ment under the bar and getting back into position for a repetition. The way of transferring weight to and from the bar, the distances to move in relation to the bar, the changes of direction which are necessary, the position of each take-off and landing as well as ways to grip and hold the bar, must all be worked out. Restraining pauses may be needed, and sudden bursts of energy and speed, and these must all follow in logical order to give whole and rhythmically satis-fying sequences of movement. The rhythm depends on the right timing of actions and when this is felt the strongly accented moments stand out in contrast to the less accented parts. These points are mastered through repetition and practice. Youngsters who are ready for such sequences are obviously fairly experienced in ways of leading from one situation to another. Some people seem to be able to feel their way logically from one event to the next, but many people may have to work out some parts of their sequences. Sometimes links are best discovered by moving in slower motion which gives time to anticipate and feel what the next step should be. When one or more solutions have been discovered, the links should be used in their proper context and at a speed which helps the rhythm of the action as a whole.

Skill in making resilient recoveries and joining these fluently with the next action is also vitally necessary in games when, having made one action, such as passing a ball, or a stroke in cricket or tennis, it is essential to recover immediately in order to move and prepare for the next event. The natural tendency is to relax after the climax, but a good games player resists this lag and recovers and prepares simultaneously, without any prolonged period of relaxation and inattention.

Timing and rhythm in action

The influence of timing on rhythm in action has already been stressed. The right timing is of paramount importance for any mis-timing breaks the rhythm and flow of movement and throws the whole action out of gear. Timing, in this sense, describes a particular moment in time when a crucial happening occurs, for example, the moment when the take-off for a jump is made, when apparatus is grasped, or in games, when the bat contacts the ball, or when the ball is released for a throw. This moment is probably the crux of skill in action. Mind, will and body all contribute to concentrating on and sensing the right timing for an action. The preparation for an action is for this very moment when accumulated energy is released to bring about the climax, in which the point of the action is accomplished (page 113). Though the climax is a moment of major importance, there are other parts of actions which have to be well timed, and in complex skills several moments depend on accurate timing. Timing in skilled action depends on when and how to place the stress, when to grasp or release apparatus, when to place the hands or other parts of the body on apparatus, when to arrest and hold movement as well as when to unbalance the body to set it in motion. In complex skills, the linking movements play an important part in getting the timing right for the chief events in the sequence of movements.

A sense for right timing in action can most easily be developed through activities in which the timing is clearly predictable. The rhythm of a swinging rope can be 'felt' and seen, and learning when to jump on to it concentrates attention on the timing of the action. Another skill, swinging forward and backward on a bar and jumping off backward to land resiliently and with balance, is a task which needs exact timing, and so does the sharp twist which turns the body over at the height of every swing in a continuous swinging movement on a single rope. This is the type of material which can be given as tasks when the teacher sees it is appropriate to stress the importance of timing in action. A sense of timing develops with the growing awareness of when in actions to do things (*when* to yield for landing, let go or arrive on apparatus, take off for a vault, or add impetus for a swing). Good timing is inextricably linked with the rhythm of action which in turn is bound up with a feeling for the flow of movement.

Many people have a very good sense of rhythm but there are some who have great difficulty in keeping a rhythm with a regular beat. Most young children get caught up in the rhythmic sound and feeling of their own hammering, stamping, clapping and other repetitive actions, and most children love to dance and jig about when they hear music which appeals to them. These repetitive rhythms are about us everywhere, even inside us, in our heart beat and breathing, so it seems strange that in spite of experience from the time of birth, there are people who have so little ability to appreciate a rhythmic beat. In dance lessons, audible stimuli through the use of percussion instruments, are used as one means of inducing a rhythmic movement response, but in gymnastics, rhythms arise in another way, through the actions themselves. Repetitive rhythms, with a metric beat, emerge as a result of repeating simple actions such as skipping, or bouncing on and off forms, or jumping from side to side over bars. These repetitive actions give rhythms with a regular pulse, but even more complex combinations of actions may, by repetition, give a similar, regular, metric rhythm. Many actions of gymnastics and other skills have a different non-metric rhythm. These action-rhythms build up, through a preparation to a climax, and die down in the recovery, and the speed and energy fluctuations make stressed and non-stressed parts. It is the balance between the working and resting phases which gives rhythmic movement its economy and harmony. People who have little feeling for repetitive rhythms often show more feeling for this freer type of rhythm, and they can move dynamically and effectively in their own personal way. The repetitive, soporific rhythms of the traditional gymnastics, taught people to keep a rhythmic beat, but it seemed almost to quell natural rhythm. The constant swinging in women's gymnastics was pleasant to do, but it did not demand much variation of dynamic movement, and some people were almost unable to change or move in a dynamic and lively way, and nor could they recognise the rhythm in the natural actions of work and play.

The importance of practice and repetition has already been stressed. Both are needed to establish the feeling of the rhythm and to clarify the exact form of any complex action. Movement memory, kinaesthetic sense and co-ordination are developed by repetition. The technical skills of athletics, swimming and diving are the means to an end, and through constant intelligent repetition a stage can be reached when performance becomes almost automatic and the performer's whole attention can be given to ways of winning and to coping with the stresses and excitement which this entails. The individual skills of educational gymnastics are not the means to an end in the same way, their chief value is in all the experience gained through learning, rather than the end product which is relatively unimportant, though the skill achieved finally gives great satisfaction and is often repeated for the sheer joy of being able to move with masterly skill (page 146f). For all such skills it is possible to practice and repeat exactly (with slight corrective variations), because external conditions do not change and are wholly predictable, and, therefore, everything depends on the performer. More adaptability and variation are needed for skills such as working with others in partner or group work (page 74), or with mobile apparatus, and in the technical skill of games. In these skills it is imperative to be able to adapt the timing, rhythm and form of actions to the myriad variations of circumstance. A clever player is always trying to mislead an opponent into mis-timing, so in tennis the length, force and speed, height and angle of shots are varied to deceive opponents. Bowlers vary their balls to trick the batsmen and goal shooters in all games try to disguise when and where the shot is going in order to upset the goalkeeper's timing.

Quality in action stems from the dynamic side of movement, quality is the outcome of what we ourselves put into movement. The way of moving depends on how one 'wills' to move, and how people feel about what they are doing. Daring and resolution will affect movement in one way, fear or nervousness in another. Interest and enjoyment, fun and humour have a tonic effect and influence the way we feel, and in turn, how we move. The dynamic side of movement is too often neglected in teaching gymnastics, and this may be caused by too great absorption by what is being done to the exclusion of all else. It may partly be accounted for because it demands understanding, feeling and awareness of movement as well as good powers of observation on the part of the teacher. Teachers who are interested in quality often inspire their classes and fire their enthusiasm. The teacher's respect for quality and individuality generally sparks off the children's interest and respect and they come to value a personal interpretation and enjoy the uniqueness of each other's movement.

The space factor in gymnastics

A distinction must be drawn between the Space *factor* of motion and other *aspects* of space. The Space factor is one of the four motion factors and it indicates a subjective, personal attitude to space which affects the way a person moves. Space aspects of movement deal with the space environment, with where movement goes through space in different levels and directions, and with the relationship of the body to the space surrounding it.

People generally show a subconscious preference in their approach to space. Some move with a feeling of *directness* which shows in the restricted, economical way they use space, moving in straight pathways through it. Others move with a greater feeling of *flexibility* and their gestures are more roundabout and unrestricted. Since these are qualitative considerations they cannot be taken into account when assessing the requirements for carrying out practical tasks which are subject to externally imposed conditions. But since people's approach to movement is influenced by their attitude to it, it inevitably affects the way they move and do things. Both a direct and a flexible approach may achieve the desired end. Compare the twisting movements and indirect pathway of a bowler delivering a googly with the directness of run, approach and delivery of many fast bowlers. Both ways of moving are needed, but people who are over-direct would gain by having greater flexibility, and conversely, the over-flexible type of person would be helped by more directness. If teachers see children with an exaggeration in either way, it might be possible to help them to gain wider experience through guiding them in the way they move when they tackle their movement problems.

Movement in gymnastics has a tendency to be direct. We often focus attention on some object and make straight for it. The rectangular room and squareness of many of the objects in it tend to give a feeling of straightness and directness. Educational gymnastics needs every kind of movement and we must see to it that there is opportunity in lessons to use flexible movement and roundabout pathways. Twisting and turning combined with all forms of locomotion can give flexibility, and movement with constantly changing directions and ways of facing, like travelling fluently over and round, in and out of people and things, with a pliant, flexible way of using the body, gives experience in using space freely and with flexibility. Jumping and leaping with whirling legs and turning, twisting body, as well as the lighter spinning, turning jumps give the same sensation of flexibility. Actions on apparatus such as swinging and twisting on ropes, twisting and wriggling in and out of window ladders, twirling jumps through bars or over apparatus can all be done in a flexible way. Such movement increases versatility and adaptability and makes people more bodily pliant.

Movement themes

Movement themes are not often used as the main subject of lessons because movement permeates action and should be stressed at all times. All the ideas which have been presented in this section should be used to enrich experience whenever the need arises. Therefore, if a class would profit by experiencing more consciously how to touch and contact things, how to propel or stop themselves, how it feels to yield to or overcome gravity, then these matters should be dealt with in the normal course of the lesson. Sometimes, however, the teacher may consider it would be beneficial, and make a more lasting impression, to spend a few lessons in concentrating on some specific Movement Theme, and if so, a Movement Theme should be chosen as the main theme.

Suggestions for possible Movement themes:

   Speed changes in various actions (combined with locomotion).

   Yielding to gravity and resisting it (combined with actions involving rising and sinking, including jumping).

   Imparting energy to propel and check the body (combined with moving and stopping).

   Continuity in movement.

When classes have a good background of experience and understanding, the following themes provide interesting subjects:

   Phrasing of movement.

   Continuity of movement.

   Imparting energy and restraining movement (combined with moving and stopping, and leaping, swinging, arriving).

   Climax in various actions.

   Timing in action.

   Rhythm in action.

   Metric and non-metric rhythms in action.

   Direct and roundabout movement.

SPACE ASPECTS OF ACTION

The use of space has not the same significance in gymnastics as in dance. Space is essentially the dancer's medium, but the intricacies of Space harmony, which are very important in dance have little significance in the practical, objective actions of gymnastics. Nevertheless, awareness of different aspects of space is important for several reasons. Accuracy of movement is increased since, in order to move with precision it is essential to judge exactly *where* to move in the space around. Versatility is also increased by the growing awareness of the possibilities of movement, and safety is another factor which is affected by the sensible and competent use of the available space. The various aspects of space are closely integrated in action but they will be considered separately for the sake of clarity. They are:

Personal space.

General space.

Direction in space.

Levels in space.

Pathway and Floor pattern.

Pathway through space and Air pattern.

and in relation to apparatus:

Height, distance and spacing.

Personal space

This is the space immediately surrounding the body, the space in which all body movements take place including everywhere that can be reached without altering the base. The centre of this sphere is the centre of the body and movement goes out from and in towards this point, round about and through it, and at all levels. Movement can also extend far from the body and take place close to it, and in the space between. The directions are rising upward and sinking down, reaching forward and stretching back, out to each side and in all intermediate directions. Awareness of all the regions in the sphere of Personal Space increases versatility and gives more scope for inventiveness.

Greater precision and accuracy are achieved when there is awareness of where in space to direct movement, and this also calls for powers of concentration and attention. To move harmoniously all parts of the body must act but the part which leads movement is particularly emphasised (page 101). The leading part takes a specific direction and this becomes the one which holds the performer's attention, for example, when stretching into a long shape, if the hands were leading, the eyes would follow the direction taken by the hands, or when jumping to make a twisted, arched shape, the important direction, at the climax, might be round-back-down, following the rear shoulder. The head is arched back and is often turned over the shoulder to follow the curve and twist of the spine, and the eyes look down behind the shoulder. (This jump can be made with a countertwist of the head so that the main stress is in an upward direction.) By making the eyes follow the important direction, the head is brought into the right relationship with the spine. The directions taken by other parts of the body are kinaesthetically felt and this means that all parts of the body participate actively to give a feeling of integration in movement.

Since all body movement takes place within the Personal space, this aspect of space should be stressed whenever a Body theme is the subject of lessons.

General space

By reaching out to the limits of the Personal space and by tilting or thrusting away from the base, movement through the General space is started. The General space is bounded by the limits of the environment. Sensible use of the general space is needed for safety, both in dashing about freely and when using, placing and arranging apparatus. Most children need guidance in how to utilise the available space because they often tend to crowd together or follow one another, sheeplike, round the room, and appear only to see straight in front, and to be quite unable to take an independent line of action. Many classes have to be taught to look at the space around them and the objects in it, and to move freely without collisions and without hindering others. Through various forms of locomotion they can gain experience of manoeuvring themselves so that they can rush about confidently, swerving, twisting, dodging, checking and stopping, according to need, and soon they become quick to see and sense the space around them.

When people become more skilful, they should be given experience of moving in a much more limited area in order to feel the restrictions of a small space and to impress upon them the need for care when moving close to others. This should then be contrasted with the feeling of moving with freedom and well spaced out, using all the room available. A well trained class will always show ability to share and use space in a sensible, considerate way and with awareness of the needs of others.

All actions involving locomotion take place in the general space and this aspect should be stressed whenever such themes are the subjects of lessons.

Directions in space

Sensible and versatile use of the general space includes moving with constantly changing directions to dodge sideways through narrow spaces, to twist and turn in and out of people and things, and to draw back or check to avoid collisions. Constant changes of direction enlarges one's horizon and overcomes blinkered and queue-minded ways of moving. There are two forms of change of direction; it can be changed by turning to face a different wall, or by moving forward, backward or sideways facing the same wall throughout. To be skilful in both these ways of moving gives greater adaptability; good games players are often adept in it. People can learn to sense, as well as see, if anyone is near them and so avoid collisions; it is a sense highly developed in blind children. Directional changes are practised in all gymnastic actions including apparatus work. Movement along or over apparatus can be made in any direction, and with a change of direction or way of facing, in the course of an action. The spaces around and between the apparatus often invite a change of direction, and it is important for safety that people should be able to twist, turn and change direction with nimbleness and agility.

Levels in space

All levels of space, high, medium and low are used in gymnastics. 'Level' in space means the relation of the body to the space above, around it and low down. High is the area of space near the top of the body and above it, low is the area close to the ground, and medium the space between these areas. One is not necessarily using a high level in space by being raised on high apparatus, because 'level in space' is also related to the body support, near the support being low, far from it, high. People should experience moving low down, close to the ground, in many different ways and directions, and on a medium level, swirling and spinning to become aware of the area of space which is neither high nor low, and they should also feel the sensation of getting high and moving on a high level, lifting, leaping and reaching up. It should always be in the back of the teacher's mind to ensure that all levels are used because movement becomes more dynamic and exciting if levels are constantly changed. The medium level is least stressed because, on the whole, it is more in keeping with gymnastics to change in an agile way from high to low, and the reverse, bounding into the air and moving close to the ground, or with the body inverted, reaching high with the feet and then tumbling down low. Apparatus is often used to enhance the sensation of flying high or to accentuate the feeling of moving low, close to it or under. In these actions movement goes through the medium level, but there are a few occasions when the medium level is stressed by skimming over the floor or over apparatus without any effort to go high or low.

Levels and directions in space should be stressed when both Body themes and themes involving locomotion, are the subject of lessons.

Pathway and floor pattern

All travelling on the floor makes a track or pathway. This is generally incidental in gymnastics, but there are occasions when the track of movement is stressed by giving tasks in which travelling is done in straight, zigzag, curved or twisted pathways. The pathway influences the movement as a whole; a straight, direct pathway would prove the most successful for the run preceding a symmetrical vault, and a curved course might be more suitable for vaults or jumps with turning. In games, bowlers affect the delivery by the type of run which is used for the preparation. The ability to use various types of pathway gives more flexibility in travelling since wavy, twisting pathways encourage pliability, and straight or angular pathways induce more direct movement.

Pathway in space and air pattern

By watching any part of the body as it moves, the pathway through space and the pattern made can be discerned. Sometimes the movement of the body as a whole is seen, for example, in diving, including diving on to and over long apparatus, or dive rolls in which the pattern of the trajectory of the body is a clear curved, rising and falling pattern. It helps some to improve their skill when they become aware of the pattern of movement through space. Sometimes the pathway made by part of the body is more significant, e.g. the pathway of the arms in swimming, or the feet leading the body to shoot through bars or over apparatus.

Height, distance and spacing of apparatus

The placing and relationship of apparatus, and the width, size, height, shape and inclination as well as possible angles of approach must be judged for successful action. These things, one assumes, are taken in at a glance, but many misjudgments could be avoided if more attention were given to it. The teacher should encourage observation, particularly of a group's own apparatus, and generally, of everything in the room as a whole. Assessment of these matters gives more awareness of the relationship of things, whether they are near or far away, behind, in front, at the side, above or below. The angle of approach can vary, and the skilful mounting and descending from apparatus sometimes depends on the right judgement of angles and spaces.

Space themes

Space themes are not often used as the main subject of lessons, but a versatile use of space is of vital importance and should be emphasised as an integral part of every lesson. The teacher might, however, feel that a few lessons concentrating on the use of space could prove beneficial in gaining or consolidating an awareness of various aspects of space. This might happen while developing themes such as 'Locomotion', 'Bending and Stretching', or 'Leg Awareness'. If the teacher realises that a wider conception of the use of space would open up new fields of movement for the class, it might be wise to change the main emphasis of the lesson in order to make this point.

Suggestions for possible Space themes:

Awareness of the General Space (in connection with Loco-motion).

Changes of direction (combined with Locomotion and Body movements).

(Awareness of the General space is generally combined with changes of direction.)

Use of various pathways of movement.

The following combined themes might be suitable for more advanced classes:

Use of Personal space and General space (combined with Locomotion and Body movements).

Turning, and planes of movement.

Movement near and far from the body (combined with Flight and Body movements).

Planning, teaching and observation

THE CONTENT, STRUCTURE AND DEVELOPMENT OF THE LESSON

A gymnastics lesson has two closely connected main parts. The first part gives experience of movement without apparatus and is designed as a preparation for the apparatus work which is the climax of the lesson. It acts as a limbering of the body in preparation for the strong and more exacting effort required later. It is also used to give experience in new aspects of movement and for repetition and practice of previous work. It helps to induce the right mood for the lesson and stimulates movement inventiveness.

Part II is the apparatus work and here the experience and knowledge gained in the first part is extended in the use of various pieces of apparatus. The lesson ends with a Final movement.

The content of the lesson is:

Part I. Floor work, roughly ⅓ of the lesson time
    Free practice for warming up
    Movement experience

Part II. Apparatus work, about ⅔ of the lesson time
    Class activities;
    and/or
    Section work
    Final movement

N B All examples used as illustration for the lesson are taken as far as possible, from one aspect of movement, the Body Theme of Bending and Stretching. This is done to show how one subject might be treated in the different stages of the lesson.

PART I Floorwork

Free practice for warming up

Children should be trained to warm up as soon as they come into the gymnasium. This free practice can take various forms:

Practice of any floorwork which particularly interests an individual;

or

Practice of some activity learnt in a previous lesson;

or

A series of movements to limber all parts of the body such as:

Springing and landing using the feet resiliently.

Bending, stretching, arching and twisting the body combined with weight transference.

Taking weight on the hands and recovering resiliently.

If the teacher is energetic and encouraging in giving training for free practice, the children will respond and no time is wasted because everyone starts work on entering the gymnasium. Young, energetic classes have a chance to 'let off steam' and are then much more ready for the lesson. Older classes which may sometimes be less eager to get started, may need more urging, but when the habit of starting work at once is formed, they work more readily if they have had time to shake off their lethargy in their own way. This part of the lesson should take only a few minutes but the teacher must prove to the class that it is an important part of the work. Help and correction should be given and comments made on the quality and standard achieved.

Movement experience

The free practice is followed immediately by the movement experience. If possible, the free practice should be merged into this part of the lesson and so avoid a sudden break. Initially the teacher selects some aspect of movement, a Theme (page 141), which will be studied for a series of lessons, and it should be one which the teacher considers will give the class the type of experience most needed at the time. The Theme will be explored so that the children get an all round experience of it.

The teacher starts by giving the class a task (page 144) to work with. Every child works individually while the teacher observes.

Soon some general advice based on these observations, will be given. This may either be directed towards helping the children to improve what they are doing or helping them to develop awareness of more aspects of the problem. For example, in a study of bending and stretching, to improve what the class is doing the children may need to be made more aware of what is involved in the subject (page 86).

In order to encourage a class to develop and explore the many possible ideas, the teacher may have to remind the children about their previous movement experience, such as supporting weight in different ways, using many directions for both bending and stretching, use of speed changes and changes of level of movement. After a thorough exploration of all possible ideas, a time for consolidation may be given. The children might be asked to invent a movement, a short sequence of events, which they can remember and repeat and practise until they have fully mastered it (page 145).

This part of the lesson should give all round movement experience and should have an effect on every part of the body. Therefore the tasks which the teacher sets should include the following activities:

Travelling. This consists of moving around using the whole space of the room, sharing it with others, and the purpose is to establish awareness of the general space.

Movement of the trunk and spine, bending, stretching, arching and twisting, in order to stress the use of the trunk in all movement, and increase awareness of the personal space.

Leaping and landing in which elevation and yielding are stressed, as well as resilience, in easy light landings and nimble weight transference.

Balance and holding the body weight in equilibrium as this trains a finer sense of balance.

The items need not be separated in the way described, in fact it is better if they are not, nor need they be taken in the order given, but each of these different aspects is needed to give sound all round bodily training and comprehensive movement preparation for the agility work on apparatus. There should be a good flow of movement throughout so that the various systems of the body are stimulated and the children are thoroughly prepared, mentally and physically, for the more exacting and strenuous demands of the apparatus work.

In first introducing a new movement theme it may be difficult to make a connection between different items, but as the theme develops this becomes possible. This lesson might start with an exploration of what is involved in bending and stretching. A first task, to discover all the directions in which the body can bend and stretch, could lead to a second task of stretching and spreading out into space to unbalance the body into travelling. This easily leads to a development of a third task of travelling and leaping with stretching away from the floor and landing with yielding to curl up and transfer weight. The shapes which resulted from the first task might now be used in the leaps, and as balances while moving on the ground. It may need several lessons to reach this point. Each separate task must be understood and experienced widely, and skill must be developed alongside versatility. For example, as soon as the leaping and landing start there will undoubtedly be need for practice in landing, and to discover what this has to do with bending and stretching. These tasks and the developments from them have the makings of several interesting sequences and the planning of them should be part of the teacher's preparation, but the tasks must not be forced through if the class shows signs of leading in other directions.

After a few lessons when the teacher has seen how the children use the apparatus, some tasks may be given in the floorwork which are a direct help for some of the apparatus work. To improve jumps with a body stretch from apparatus, the floorwork might include high jumps with many different ways of stretching, followed by appropriate landings and rolls which lead into further stretching movements in the recoveries. Such experience should develop more awareness of bodily movement as well as giving ideas which could be used in the jumps from apparatus.

PART II Apparatus Work

Section work

This is the climax of a gymnastics lesson and should, therefore, always be included. The class is divided into groups of four or five people and each group is given apparatus to work with. Generally, a group should work at a given piece until the teacher makes a change thus ensuring that everyone gets the necessary variety of experience. The groups should be small so that everyone can be actively employed all the time, for rest periods are not necessary in a well planned lesson. More than five or six in a group often leads to queueing for turns and this can break the flow of the lesson, which makes the pace drop and can produce boredom.

The grouping should normally be according to height as this makes the adjustment of the apparatus, especially bars, much simpler. Also, if partners have to help or support one another, it is often better that they should be about the same height and weight. But there are occasions when free grouping is viable, especially for more experienced classes, which may be interested in Group work, and wish to work with friends.

At times some regimentation is helpful to a class. First year children coming to a new school have many strange and over-whelming experiences which affect them, and it may be that ready made organisations can relieve them of one burden and offer them a certain stability for a few weeks. To belong to a set group and use fixed Section places in the room before starting the apparatus work, can give a short breathing space and help to promote a sense of order. Adolescent classes, who are inexperienced through not having had a teacher earlier in their secondary school lives, or classes which are disintegrated for other reasons, can also benefit if this part of the lesson is arranged for them so that they do not have to make decisions and think for themselves all the time. It is essential that the teacher should get to know the youngsters as soon as possible, and thereby be in a position to judge when a class can be expected to take responsibility, and when it would be better to give more help.

So that lessons provide variety, ensure all round activity, prove exciting and stimulating, the apparatus work should, if possible, include the following:

   a. Hanging, climbing and swinging.

   b. Jumping and vaulting.

   c. Tumbling, rolling and somersaulting.

   d. Balancing and sliding.

These activities may be combined but the lesson should give opportunity for each type. In each of these activities, the whole body is actively working, but in a. the arms, shoulders and upper part of the body are taking the main strain. In b. the legs and hips are most strongly used, and in c. the trunk and spine should be particularly stressed, and in d. general control of balance and co-ordination are most emphasised. Progression from section to section should be carefully planned as this will help to ensure that no one is strained or over tired and that everyone gets all round experience. A short period at the end of the lesson can be set aside for free choice, when all go to the section which most interests them. Another ending to the apparatus work, especially with competent classes, is to send them round the room, leaping through bars, jumping over boxes and horses, swinging up on to things, to test their skill and adaptability in unrehearsed, spontaneous situations. It also gives the teacher an opportunity to assess the general skill, versatility and attack of the group, and this will give guidance for the planning of future lessons.

The apparatus should be arranged so that the space of the room is well used and so that people do not get in each other's way. The planning must take place round the fixed apparatus, and the portable apparatus can be put in the available spaces. Some apparatus, which should be approachable from any angle, will need a wide area of space around it, and corners of the room are useful for this. Other pieces, which may be used with a more direct approach, will only need a long, narrow space, such as the space in the centre of the room between bars. An interesting, well arranged room with plenty of variety and apparatus of various height, gives a sense of harmony and at the same time a feeling of excitement and stimulation, and such psychological effects must be taken into account. The way the apparatus is handled is extremely important and the teacher should always bear this in mind when planning Part II of the lesson. (See Handling, page 71).

As in Part I of the lesson, problems to solve are also given as a starting point in the apparatus work, but the very first thing to be done is to allow a short period of free practice. This gives the children a chance to get the feeling of the apparatus and to use it in a way which is fitting for them at the moment. All that is necessary is a few trial turns. The teacher then gives the class more specific tasks. Experience proves that when working with a new theme, the quickest, clearest and most practical way is to give the same task to be solved at each section. The task must be related to the subject of the lesson, e g 'Use the apparatus as you choose but discover when and how you bend and stretch'. Tasks with a common factor can be used at every stage of experience. Advanced classes will be working with more difficult subjects and more complicated arrangements of apparatus and, therefore, a general task should prove satisfactory even for experienced classes. To give a different task at each section is a waste of time, causes confusion, makes things much more difficult for the teacher and also distracts from the clarity of the lesson.

When different tasks are given to each group, children listen only to the first task and have little idea of what to do when they change to the next section. Set tasks, different for each group, also tend to limit the scope of exploration and should, therefore, only be introduced at a later stage. Such tasks are more necessary if the class's explorations lead to little result. They should be used at a stage when the specific purpose is to limit certain groups and compel them to get an experience which the teacher considers is valuable for them.

The class is taught during the apparatus work in much the same way as in the first part of the lesson. Teaching can be individual or general and is directed to widening the scope of the work or to making the youngsters more aware of how they are moving and so improving the style and quality of the work. (Page 145.)

Class activities

This is another way of taking apparatus work and can be done when there is enough of any one type of apparatus, e g bars, ropes, forms, mats, wall bars, so that every group can have the same. The teacher uses this method for various reasons:

> To make a link between the floorwork and the apparatus work. Apparatus such as forms or mats can be used, for the first experience, to clarify how principles learnt in the floorwork can be exploited also in the apparatus work.

> To introduce new apparatus to beginners, e g handling and use of bars.

> To teach some basic skill to a whole class at the same time. Such skills should be stepping-stones to further progress and should be suitable for the whole class, e g:

>> Jumps from forms, with single or double take-off and a variety of landings.

>> 'Arriving' on forms or saddles, tilting off to roll away and recover.

>> Body waves under bars or at wall bars.

> For correction of faults common to many in the class, such as incomplete push to lift the body in vaulting,

>> incomplete pull to lift the body in jumping on to ropes or bars,

>>> head not tucked in which spoils the rounded shape for rolling.

N B   All the examples are forms of bending and stretching.

This way of taking the apparatus work enables the teacher to make the points clear to the whole class. With beginners it may prove helpful to take all the apparatus in this way for a number of lessons. It is possible to take several activities, one after another, and so still give variety of experience.

A stage between class activities and section work is to have two activities in progress. Half the class, still divided into small groups, might use ropes or bars, while half use forms and mats. Then, each group changes place with a group in the other half. A further stage is to divide each half class into three or four sections and duplicate the apparatus, such as two sets each of:

Forms inclined on wall bars.

Ropes used with bars.

Horse or box with mattress and a form.

Each half class changes round the three sections in its own part of the room. This is a very satisfactory way of arranging apparatus for large classes when lessons are short, and also for classes which have only one lesson or less, in the week.

Class activities should, however, be considered as a preliminary stage of apparatus work and only be used for the reasons already given. Section work is the aim for the climax of the lesson because it asks much more of a class. Greater self-discipline is needed, more initiative, independence and sense of responsibility are to be expected.

Final movement

After the apparatus has been cleared away the class should be gathered together by a final movement which will help also to calm them down before dismissal. This can be preceded by a short period of free practice until everyone is ready, and should be followed by a movement which brings about upright balanced carriage and good poise.

THEMES FOR LESSONS

Lessons are built up around themes, and a theme is a concept of movement which forms the core, or main subject of the lesson. This central idea is a unifying factor which clarifies the purpose and gives direction to lessons. Themes enable teachers to build their work systematically and give them a way of making consistent progress. There need be no hard and fast rules about the ideas which can be exploited as themes and there is nothing to prevent teachers who understand what they are doing, from creating their own ideas to develop as the subjects of lessons, but they must be thoughtfully chosen according to the abilities, experience and interests of each class.

Themes are drawn from the subject matter of gymnastics. (Part II.) There are various types:

Action themes	are based on the main actions of gymnastics.
Body themes	are based on the body movements which occur in actions, and the Bodily aspect of action offers suggestions for such themes.
Movement themes	are drawn from the Dynamic aspects of action.
Space themes	deal with the spatial aspects of action.
Composite themes	stress more than one aspect, e g bending and stretch.ng with weight transference, or, Flight stressing Body Shape.

Even though a theme gives a lesson a main stress this does not exclude other aspects from the teaching. Every relevant aspect is used in developing the main theme in order to give wide, all round experience and understanding of what is involved in the theme.

Action themes are always supported by movement (bodily and dynamic aspects), and by various space stresses. An example may clarify how every aspect of movement is used in developing an Action theme:

Theme	Locomotion
Purpose	To investigate many ways of moving through space
Stage	Secondary school beginners

Points which are developed through a series of lessons:

> Use of the general space.
>
> Use of all directions.
>
> Movement on straight and twisted pathways.
>
> Movement through various levels.
>
> Use of various speeds.
>
> Practice of moving and stopping.
>
> Experiments in moving on all parts of the body:
> legs only, hands and feet and on other parts.

This Action theme is developed through ideas which have space stresses, dynamic stresses and a bodily emphasis. An example of the development of a Body theme (Bending and Stretching) illustrated the 'Structure, Content and Development of the Lesson' (page 133). The actions of jumping, travelling and balancing were all included. These actions were selected and given as tasks in the lesson because all clearly demonstrated the need for bending and stretching. Suggestions were also made to show how the dynamic and space aspects were used to contribute quality and versatility in movement. Movement and Space themes are less practical as themes in their own right, but they are sometimes used for a few consecutive lessons in order to focus attention on some particular matter. For instance, while developing an Action or a Body theme, the teacher may observe that the class shows little skill or understanding in matters such as the use of space, or of changes of speed. If so, this may be the sign to change the emphasis and make one of these subjects the theme of the lesson. The material of the lesson need not be radically altered but the stress is changed. This will, however, mean a careful review of the material and possibly some changes should be made so that the point of the new theme is very clear. To make such a change is an opportunity to deal with familiar material in a new way and in greater depth.

Themes develop in two main directions, one to give a broad, general experience of what is involved in the theme, and the other to improve the quality of what is done. The change of emphasis described above might have been necessitated by the class getting too far ahead with what it is possible to do, without at the same time, enough attention being paid to how to do it well. These two sides should be stressed equally. One gives a great variety of activity, and the other gives quality in movement.

Selecting themes and choosing material

Themes are selected for classes on grounds of their needs. This and other matters (see Observation) are assessed by the teacher who must be able to observe accurately and have an understanding both of children and movement. This knowledge is essential if a wise choice of work is to be made. Having selected a theme, the teacher prepares and plans work on the lines suggested for planning lessons Material must be chosen, and tasks be given which make the main purpose apparent early in the lesson. Some teachers prefer to plan the apparatus work first. This means planning tasks suitable for each type of apparatus work (page 137). Part I of the lesson can then be planned, and this should include actions which give varied experience (page 135) and which lead up to the apparatus work. The ideas which are developed in this part of the lesson should also stimulate movement inventiveness ready for Part II. The preparatory work should be a general exploration for the first few lessons, because it is more important in the early stages to make the purpose clear, and to discover all the ideas connected with the theme. If the preparatory work is too directly applicable to the apparatus work, many enjoyable and exciting movements on the floor may be lost. For this reason many teachers prefer to plan Part I first and allow the apparatus work to develop from this. A more direct link between the floor work and the apparatus tends to grow as the material becomes more familiar to the class. The exploratory stage passes gradually to the stage of selection and consolidation.

Duration of themes

The amount of time spent working on a theme depends entirely on how it develops, on the interest of the children and what they are still getting out of the work. An Action theme such as Travelling (page 33) covers a very large field of possibilities and could easily be profitable for about half a term. Whether there are one or two lessons a week does not matter, for in any case a change of subject might be advisable after half a term in order to bring new life and inspiration to the lessons. Body themes may or may not be long enduring. In themselves they are not strictly functional; body movement is only one aspect of functional action. If many exciting actions develop from the investigations of the theme, interest will certainly last and continue to have value for the class. Movement and Space themes may only be profitable for two or three lessons, particularly at the elementary and intermediate stages, for reasons already given. At an advanced level, knowledgeable people can work for long periods on themes such as 'Rhythm and Timing', 'Repetitive rhythms and Action rhythms', 'Phrasing and continuity' or 'Turning and Planes of movement'.

Progression from one theme to the next

This, too, depends on the needs of the class. These generally become apparent to the teacher as the current theme is being taught. How and why one changes the emphasis and adopts a Movement or a Space theme has already been discussed. There can be no hard and fast rules in such matters, since whatever the teacher considers will best contribute to the class's experience and understanding, will be the best answer. Several themes deal with basic material (see Progression, page 150) and, therefore, in making a change, it generally would not matter which theme were chosen next. By selecting themes in an order such as: an Action theme, followed by a short consolidation period with a Space or Movement theme, or both, followed by a Body theme, and then another Action theme, is one way of building up and making systematic progress. The teacher is the person who is in the position to decide if a particular scheme would work in practice. In any case, it cannot definitely be decided far in advance, because it may prove that there is no need for the next pre-planned step.

Exploration and selection of tasks

All new situations are approached through tasks of exploration which are given by the teacher for the class to work out. The wording of these tasks must be very clear so that everyone knows what to do. Words such as 'Find out', 'Discover' or 'Invent' will probably be used to introduce new work because these lead to the exploration and experimentation which gives such interest and versatility in good educational gymnastics, but the words of the task must also include an action because this clarifies what is to be done, e g 'Discover ways of *travelling* on hands and feet', or 'Find ways of helping your partner to *jump*'. (N B The examples used hereafter show developments of these two ideas.) As soon as the class starts to work, the teacher observes in order to discover the next and most profitable step. One step is to extend the range of what is happening, and a way of doing this is to remind the class of any previous movement experience (varied use of hands and feet, changes of speed and direction, moving and stopping), or it may be even more important to improve the quality of what is happening. Expansion and improvement are both necessary, even at the exploratory stage. When the teacher is satisfied that the class has gained all it can from this, it is taken on to the next stage.

Selection and development

In the floorwork new tasks are given in which:

> Everyone is asked to select a skill for intensive practice (this should be something of interest discovered in the exploratory stage).
>
> *or*
>
> The teacher makes the selection and the whole class practises the task set, e g 'Practise ways of coming down from your hands, yielding softly when you land'.
>
> *or*
>
> The class is given the task of composing a sequence of movement based on the explorations.

These sequence tasks must also be carefully worded. The words should conjure up a picture of logical possibilities, e g 'Link several cartwheels; start with small ones and work up to a final big one', or, 'The first partner make three jumps helped by the second, and then change. Everything must be linked together so that there are no breaks in the continuity of movement.' The tasks are always only a beginning; the teacher must be ready both to hold back and let the children try on their own, and also, to step in to help and guide.

The apparatus work develops in a slightly different way. While exploring, some people discover skills which interest them, and immediately set about mastering them. Others seek and experiment for longer periods, and later select one specific action to tackle in greater depth. When the stage is reached of forming and practising a specific action or sequence of movement, there are various processes to go through in order to achieve skill:

> Each child must decide what to do, and having done this, start to practise and try to make the point of the action clear. (At this stage there are people who need the teacher's help and encouragement to get off the mark. Tentative efforts and first tries are sometimes too easily abandoned, but if the teacher can help at this moment, something may come of the attempt. The teacher must not hold back for too long from helping people who are at a loss. Two or three possible ideas can be suggested, to get them started, and they can

select one which appeals. Once they do start, a major obstacle is overcome.)

The action must be repeated until it is clearly remembered and the general feeling of it is established.

The child can then begin to look more analytically, and with the teacher's guidance or the help of a partner, begin to clarify in more detail the most relevant of the following points:

What the body is doing, as a whole, or which parts are most stressed in various phases of the action.

Where exactly parts of the body, and the body as a whole, are going. The exact gesture and placing of the next weight bearing part is often important.

How the movement is being done. The rhythm as a whole must be established and this means discovering which parts have to be more, or less, stressed, and how the timing of the action affects the whole.

Relationships of partners (or groups) pose all the complexities of discovering how to work in with others.

Sometimes one of these aspects is more important than others and, therefore, the teacher must watch to find out how best to help. Some may need help to find ways of linking the phrases of their sequences of movement, both in the floor and apparatus work. They must be helped to discover where and why they break down and how they can logically bridge the gap. Ability to anticipate what is to happen next often overcomes such difficulties. The recovery from one event can be adjusted to flow into and become the preparation for the next. Youngsters should be taught to review their sequences as a whole and have a clear beginning, a middle and an end.

While the youngsters are working to clarify and shape their actions, the teacher observes and assesses where help is needed most. Individuals may need help, which can be given directly through correction, or through a demonstration by the teacher. The teacher's leading questions may also be an aid in resolving many difficulties, but such questions should be answered in movement, not words. One group might need help, and in this case the teacher should be prepared to offer advice, and if necessary, contribute ideas. A group can also be given help in observation, in ways of helping one another and in clarification of the principles of what they are doing.

Much is gained by working to accomplish a high standard in

skills and sequences. People enjoy the sense of achievement gained by working to the limits of their ability. The repetition and practice which is needed develops movement memory, improves co-ordination, and through the elimination of ineffectual and faulty movement, habits of good movement become established and gymnastic skills achieved. If the skills themselves were of primary importance, and the purpose was to train children to become gymnasts with a repertoire of skills, then the skills could be taught directly, as techniques, which would be a much simpler and quicker way to reach the goal. But much more important than this is what the youngsters gain from the learning process itself. It may take longer to reach the same visible results, but the means are so much more important than the end. The purpose of teaching in this more difficult and exacting manner is that through it children are learning in a way which will enable them, with ever growing understanding to take more part in teaching themselves. The teaching is given through principles which youngsters can understand, put into practice and relate to other situations. The same principles and processes are reiterated constantly in lessons; the children come to understand the underlying structure of their work. Where the teacher takes the same classes for games, athletics or swimming, there is further opportunity to emphasise the movement principles underlying the structure of skilled action. One could reasonably expect that children who have had a sound and consistent movement education should be able to approach any movement situation with considerable understanding. People with reasonably good intelligence should, through their education in movement, be able to:

observe movement with understanding and quickly grasp the essence of what is happening.

imitate accurately the movement of others.

control their bodies and move in agile and versatile ways and show adaptability.

sense when and where the stress in an action should be and have feeling for rhythm and timing.

control the flow of movement and vary the speed, energy and direction as they wish.

Therefore when they want to learn something new, they have many 'tools' with which to start. The capacity to respond, naturally varies with innate ability, interest and intelligence, but the opportunity is there for a unified approach to physical education. Teachers must naturally always be ready to help children to understand the relationship of one thing to another, and they must be discriminating about the timing and the way in which they put things over. There is danger of over-intellectualising and so ruining spontaneity and killing joy. In movement one must often try first and think while doing, or after, and thereby become aware through a real situation and not a theoretical, hypothetical one.

PROGRESSION

There are several possible starting points in this form of gymnastics. In any subject the starting point must be related to previous experience and even where there is no knowledge of gymnastics, every school child has had experience of moving. We have all been through the developmental stages of wriggling, crawling, walking, climbing, running and jumping, and all children coming to secondary schools can do these things. Some are already very skilful while others show limitations, and this depends, in part, on the opportunities they have had, and used. The starting point must also be related to the stage of maturity and ability to understand, as well as interest and, therefore, how one starts with a group of lively, unsophisticated first year children is very different from the approach to more mature, worldly-wise beginners of adolescent stage. On the whole, the former group are very energetic and still have childlike qualities. They show interest in everything, insatiable curiosity, readiness to learn and try anything, and willingness to take anything on trust. The latter group are generally much more critical and in many respects much more conservative; they are more self-conscious and unwilling to commit themselves until they have complete trust in their teacher. Two such different groups must obviously be approached in different ways, and the material chosen for the younger ones is unlikely to be suitable for the older group.

Work built on previous experience generally helps to give security and confidence. Whatever a class is asked to do should, at first, be similar to things they have done before. Therefore, if an older class is accustomed to being led by the teacher throughout the lesson, or to having only apparatus work in their lessons, they must gradually be introduced to new ways, and they should naturally be given the reasons for the changes. This is particularly important when a new teacher first meets an older class. They may not be so ready to follow a new lead unless their confidence is gained and the teacher fires their interest. Intelligent people are interested in discussing what and how they gain from gymnastics, and it is not generally difficult to convince them of the benefits to themselves. In time they should also come to understand how their movement experience will stand them in good stead in their daily lives and could be a help to them in any new sport they wish to take up.

During the secondary school stage the development of children follows a clear pattern. Boys and girls mature at different rates and sex differences become more marked, therefore, the way of approach to boys and girls might not take the same form. The suggestions about progression which follow, are made with girls in mind.

Most girls entering secondary schools have reached the beginning of adolescence and yet the outlook and interests of many first and second year girls is still revealed in refreshing eagerness and spontaneity. The changes of adolescence are at their height in the middle school and the girls are growing up fast. At this stage they are sometimes unpredictable and moody, and it may be difficult to interest them. As they reach the senior forms, they generally become more stable and responsible, and their interests again change, being directed more outward, and to post-school life. Progression in a school gymnasium course must take into account all these factors. The suggestions given below assume a steady and consistent course, but where this is not the case, it is essential that the teacher judges the situation and adapts it accordingly.

Elementary stage (early adolescent period)

Many children coming from the primary schools have had experience of dance and gymnastics, but others have had few opportunities. The teacher's first task is to get to know the children, assess their ability and discover as much as possible about them and their previous experience. In the initial stages, the new school, the fully equipped gymnasium and the new teacher will make things feel strange and exciting to all the children. Children and teacher have much to discover together before settling down to a regular programme. Once under way, much ground can be covered at this eager, willing stage. The work should be exciting, adventurous and playlike, and through it the teacher should aim at helping the children to gain control of themselves. Themes connected with locomotion, jumping and simple balance skills, as well as elementary themes on bending, stretching and twisting which will give more specific awareness of the body, are the most suitable. Various qualities of movement and many aspects of space should be experienced in conjunction with this work. Simple movement terms should be used which should gradually come to have more specific meaning for the children.

All the apparatus with the exception of springboards and trampettes should be used during the first year, but arrangements of apparatus should be kept simple. On the whole, apparatus which is easily moved should be used in the first few lessons. Everything is exciting, so there is no need, in the early stages, to take out vaulting boxes and horses, which are clumsy to handle and likely to cause queueing for turns, or bars, which need careful management. The children should first be led to discover the many possible uses of the different types of apparatus, e g ropes can be used for swinging, climbing, somersaulting, turning and hanging upside down, lifting the body high, spinning and much more which they discover. They explore further if they are reminded of their movement experience of previous lessons or of Part I of the current lesson.

Necessary technique must be taught so that no one is hurt or hampered by lack of it, but versatility, attack and spirit are more important than technical skill, so technique must not be over-stressed. The main aim should be to lay a broad foundation of general skill and to develop monkey-like agility and versatility with safety and confidence. If this stage is missed it may be very difficult to make it good at a later stage.

In the next stage more stress is placed on mastering simple self-invented skills and developing better technique. The skills are those selected after exploration, and the techniques are those needed for skilled execution of the chosen actions. The techniques are also taught in order to establish good habits of movement. Much leaping and jumping should be included for if people do not 'fly' at this stage and earlier, they are unlikely to enjoy it later. Youngsters enjoy being skilful and will work very hard to master skills which interest them, therefore the opportunity should be seized to increase bodily skill in further development of themes on twisting and turning, bending and stretching, also with wheeling actions and body waves. Specific themes such as Leg Awareness may do much, at the right time, to increase awareness and give control. The limbs grow fast in early adolescence and the change may, for a time, disturb co-ordination. Balancing skills are also enjoyed but should not be overdone. They demand control and improve co-ordination, but they may be very taxing at this stage of 'unbalance'.

Partner work appeals and should be part of every lesson. Partners can be taught to coach one another (see Observation, page 164) as well as working together in joint actions. Partner work is another way of gaining more precision, but the type of work should be chosen with care to be sure it gives the experience needed by the class at the time. Well chosen partner work can be very absorbing and, therefore, an aid to concentration which is sometimes not very good at this stage.

All the apparatus should be used. Springboards and trampettes can be introduced, first for free jumps (see order of progression in

'Flight', page 49) and later with vaulting apparatus. New arrangements and combinations of apparatus often stimulate interest.

The elementary 'grammar' and 'vocabulary' of movement should be mastered by the end of the lower school period. Skill in observation should be developing and the children should have reached a stage where they can profitably coach one another in clear points given by the teacher. They should also have a large repertoire of their own skills as well as a number common to the whole class.

Intermediate stage (middle adolescent period)

Where training in the first two years has been well built up and thorough, there is every reason to believe that progress in this period can be steady. The teacher may have to cope with a change of outlook and a more critical and questioning attitude. She must be prepared for this, and be reasonable, and show consideration, patience and a sense of humour. Spirited, fickle people at this stage of development can be a real challenge and nothing is more rewarding for a teacher than to win their respect and confidence.

Many girls lose interest in the agile, vigorous skills of the previous age and so grow out of the tomboyish stage. But there are always some typical 'doers' whose nimbleness, natural exuberance and sense of fun continue to find outlet in such skills, and all must be catered for.

Girls who have worked from the beginning on the lines suggested will have mastered the basic elements of movement and gained considerable understanding. For this reason the character of Part I of the lesson may change. The girls enjoy partner work, therefore more of this can be included in the floorwork, and since they have the knowledge, it will be easier for them to compose sequences of movement, and through these gain more precision. Towards the end of this period, concentration improves and the girls work hard to master movement sequences either individually or with partners or groups. They know how to build sequences and understand something of the structure of action. The teacher can help them to become more aware of timing and rhythm in action, and help them to clarify where to put the stress. They enjoy rhythmic movement and, therefore, they should be given tasks both for floor work and apparatus work, in which they construct rhythmical sequences of jumps, vaults, swings on ropes or bars, waves with partners or under bars, and jumps along or through bars. These can also be individual, partner or group actions. This is a new and interesting way of using previously acquired skill.

Balance activities appeal and actions based on tilting or thrusting the weight off-balance, catching it and recovering equilibrium, all increase awareness of balance and, if the point is made, help to develop a feeling of poise. The teacher should be sure that such activities are suitable for the class. If they are at a very uncontrolled stage, balance activities can make them self-conscious and giggly, but if they are showing signs of gaining control, balance activities can be most successful. They are absorbing and satisfying since they give a feeling of wholeness and integration because attention is focused on control of the whole body.

Progression in apparatus work is made by giving new combinations of apparatus. Tracks can be made more complex, heights of apparatus increased and distances to be bridged, made greater. Longer sequences of actions can be expected. More partner and group work can be used and groups may enjoy making their own arrangements of apparatus, but this should always be carefully controlled by the teacher. There is danger of making complex arrangements for the sake of complexity, so that is difficult to work purposefully on it. What is done on the apparatus is always more important than the complexity of the arrangement.

An interesting development at this stage is the eagerness to work together in groups, and this is to be encouraged but not overdone. Much ineffectual work and silly stunts are done in the name of 'Group work' and such a waste of time is to be avoided. Well selected group tasks, at the right moment, are helpful and stimulating in a positive way (see Group work, page 81). The type of themes that are suitable at this stage are: Action themes based on Locomotion and Flight, Balancing skills, 'Arriving', and the simpler aspects of 'On- and Off-balance'. These will naturally be developed in a new way making use of all the skill and experience so far gained. The elementary body themes of bending, stretching and twisting can be developed into themes based on Body Shape, Symmetry and Asymmetry of the Body in movement, and Simultaneous and Successive movement of the body. Care must be taken with the presentation of the two latter ideas that they do not become an academic exercise. It is essential that the teacher is sure that the girls have a sound grasp, both in skill and understanding, and can take these ideas in their stride and see the point of them.

Physical activity is urgently needed at this stage when there are such great physical changes taking place. Some physiologists maintain that exercise which stimulates all the systems of the body is essential for the proper and full development of the organs and glands. Apart from the great physical need for activity, the main purpose in this period is to maintain interest and consolidate all previous work, and to tide over a period of instability. The main progress should be in development of rhythmical sense, poise, flow of movement and group work, all matters of vital interest at this stage. If opportunity could be offered for a choice of activity towards the end of this period, it would be ideal, for there are girls who would gain more from dance than gymnastics. Dance has much more to give in Group Work than gymnastics, but in schools which have no dance, gymnastics can do something to encourage group feeling and interest in working with others.

Advanced stage (later adolescent period)

General interests at this stage are more formed and more diverse, and interest in physical education varies greatly. Some girls never lose interest, some regain lost interest and a few have very little, if any. It would be most reasonable at this stage to give more free choice, and where practicable introduce activities which might be of interest after leaving school. Since activity is so vital for well being, everyone should participate regularly in some form or other. Where choice is allowed there are always some girls who select gymnastics. This is generally, but not always, because they are very skilful and enjoy all types of agility. Progression should depend on the ability and interests of the group. Some groups would develop more ways of working together, others enjoy more intricate individual skills. The teacher might well teach some of the Olympic-type skills which the girls have not discovered for themselves, or she might invite them to try skills of her own invention.

Most girls would find it interesting to have a few lessons which sum up and collect together knowledge which would be useful to them when they leave school. Girls who are leaving school to go to sedentary work, into factories or shops, to College or University, should understand how to keep themselves in good condition, how to stimulate or enliven themselves or relax and calm themselves down, how to correct their posture, how to walk, sit or stand and move economically. They should also know how to work all their joints and how to affect any part of their body as they wish, so that they can combat tensions, cramps and stiffnesses. They would be interested in understanding how to do the everyday jobs of lifting, carrying and other household tasks, with economy and ease. They could also be helped to become more discerning and skilful in observation, and more fully aware of how to set about the mastery of new skills. This way of working should teach people to teach themselves; it gives them the knowledge which they can use for whatever purpose they wish.

The themes which are suitable for advanced classes are the same as for the intermediate group but naturally developed in a way which exploits the skill and understanding of the girls. More combined themes can be interesting to work out, themes such as On- and Off-balance with Flight, Turning with Locomotion and Flight, Locomotion and Balance, Simultaneous and Successive movement with Balance, and movement themes such as 'Preparation – Action – Recovery', 'Climaxes in action', 'Rhythm in action' and 'Timing in action'.

Girls who have had an unbroken course in physical education from first to last year at school, with a good and interested teacher, should surely be physically educated. No ordinary physical situation should cause them doubt or fear for they have the security of knowledge and the confidence of skill.

Planning a scheme of work

To be sure of making steady progress a teacher must plan a scheme of work. It need not be planned in any great detail as that is taken care of in planning the actual lessons. A year's scheme might cover several Action themes, some Body themes, some Movement and Space themes. At the elementary stage the dynamic and space aspects of action will mainly be covered in connection with Action and Body themes (page 141), but at the intermediate stage, themes of short duration, based on these aspects, might prove profitable. At an advanced level more Space and Movement themes can be included because girls who have reached this stage have a good understanding of movement.

The reason for selecting any theme is related to the ability of a class to understand the concepts on which the theme is based. This power to comprehend is more important than physical ability though naturally this is considered, together with the extent of the movement experience of the class. Physical ability varies from very high to low in the same class, but a well selected theme gives every girl a chance of working to her limits at her own level, and as a result she gains more conscious control and mastery and at the same time, an understanding of the underlying principles of the theme.

Teaching through themes is a way of building up experience and knowledge which is cumulative, because every theme and all the experience gained from each, feeds all subsequent work. Some themes are recurrent but progression is made by incorporating all the knowledge and experience gathered in the intervening period. Repetitions are always made with a new emphasis. Various forms of Flight should be part of the scheme of work for every stage. At an elementary stage, safe landings are of primary importance, so leaping and jumping and learning to receive the weight should be stressed. When this theme recurs the emphasis might be to pay more attention to ways of taking off and different types of landing, including yielding and buoyant ways, or the stress might be concerned with Body Shape in the flight, but the new emphasis would depend on the stage of experience reached and current needs. Much groundwork of bending, stretching and twisting, and of the dynamic and spatial aspects of action should have been covered by this stage, therefore, this knowledge must all be utilised in developing the new ideas. At a yet later stage, when the girls have a further store of experience and much more skill, still more exacting versions of Flight, such as Flight combined with Arriving to Balance, or On- and Off-balance with Flight, will stretch even the ablest to their limits. Progression in recurrent themes is indicated at the end of each section describing the main actions of gymnastics (pages 37, 54, 67). Further suggestions of possible themes are given at the end of each part in the section on Movement (pages, 106, 124, 130) and from these two sources it is possible to draw up an outline scheme of work for the elementary, intermediate and advanced stages. The course of progress can be looked upon as zigzag paths between theme and theme, chosen from Action themes, Body, Space and Movement themes, while the whole pattern moves in a spiral course coming back and recrossing the path of many themes and the ideas previously covered.

It is most important to keep careful and detailed records of work which show:

> Themes used and the special stress made.
>
> Apparatus used and types of tasks given.
>
> Partner work done.
>
> Training given in observation.

A record becomes a scheme in retrospect and it can be a valuable document to pass on to a successor. A great many schoolgirls are suffering from a constant change of teacher and a lack of continuity in their work. A clear record passed on to a successor may help to alleviate this difficulty as a new teacher need not go to a class quite ignorant of their experience, but whatever she learns from the records, she must still observe acutely, draw her own conclusions and plan her work for herself.

OBSERVATION AND TEACHING

Skill in observation and the ability to react to what is seen is the key to good teaching. There are several aspects of observation and all are important if one is to be a successful teacher. In a general way, one must be able to observe people, for in this way one learns to recognise how they feel and think and why they react as they do. Movement must be observed accurately for without this skill it is not possible to judge what step to take next or how to go on to improve the work. Children must be taught to observe for it enables them to understand and recognise good movement. If they can observe well it is also a great help to the teacher both from the coaching and safety angle. Safety depends, to a large extent, on good observation by both teacher and children.

Wyld's dictionary gives a definition of the word 'Observe' as 'To consider carefully, and with concentrated attention, whether with eye or ear', and goes on in further definitions to mention becoming aware and becoming conscious. These are exactly the qualities and processes which are needed for penetrating observation. One could go even further and say that observation involves all our senses including an extra sense, intuition. All faculties of mind and senses are alerted when we observe well, and all are ready to respond to what is seen, heard or felt. Observation is clearly part of ordinary living for we are doing it all the time, but success depends to a great extent on interest; physical education teachers must train themselves to direct their looking, because so much in good teaching depends on it.

Observing people

It is essential for a teacher to be vitally interested in people and able to observe them consciously and with full awareness. Observation can give essential information about individuals as well as knowledge about classes. The stage of development can be assessed, and one finds that this is by no means uniform. In a class of the same chronological age great variations will be seen. These facts must be taken into consideration in planning the work for a class. The interests, needs and capabilities can also be judged, and a teacher new to a class will soon be able to detect much about the previous experience, both of the class and individuals. A class's eagerness, or lack of it, will reveal if the choice of work meets the needs of the children, and it is also a clue for how to continue. Observation may prove that work started can profitably continue on the same lines, or there may be indication that it would be wiser to make a change; when and how to progress also becomes clear. Past experience is revealed by the degree of understanding shown by the group, by the way people behave and their relationships with one another as well as by their attitude to authority.

In a more personal way, the teacher can learn to understand individual children through observing them perceptively, and by using imagination as well, it is possible to recognise fears and inhibitions and possibly to avert them by giving people more security and confidence. Joys and triumphs also need recognition and children like to share them. Some children need encouragement, appreciation and recognition above all else, while others may at times, need challenging and spurring to get the best from themselves. It is only by observing children's behaviour and reactions that a teacher can truly assess these things. This type of observation is not confined to the infrequent meetings of class with teacher but goes on all the time. It is part of the life of an interested teacher to look at the children at every opportunity, as one meets them in corridors, in their breaks and out of school. So much can be discovered in these 'off guard' moments which are helpful to teachers in the whole process of education.

Genuine contact with children depends on real concern for them. A first proof of this is that the teacher can identify a child by name. A name can instantly make a child feel recognised, a real person who matters to the user of the name. Praise, encouragement, help or correction is always much more potent if it can be given by name to a specific person. Knowing names is also vitally important if there are any disciplinary problems; the use of the right name at the proper moment can do much to steady or restrain anyone bent on mischief. A teacher should aim to address every child by name in every lesson, and it is the apparently colourless, innocuous, average people who tend to go unseen, therefore, special efforts must be made to notice them and draw them out. The teacher also proves interest by remembering things about the children, personal things as well as happenings in the lesson. All this may, at first, seem difficult when the class is large and the activity so diverse, but practice and experience in observation bring their rewards.

Teachers must not forget that children too can observe, and indeed do so. Consciously or sub-consciously they take in a great deal about the people they meet. They readily sense negative qualities such as nervousness or disinterest, but they are also receptive to positive qualities such as enthusiasm, hard work, constancy and integrity. Young people are influenced all the time by what they observe, the attitude, behaviour, manners, appearance, mode of address and example of the people about them. Sometimes their responses may be strange and unexpected, but nevertheless, the power of observation of sensitive, perceptive youngsters is a factor which must be reckoned with in teaching.

Observing movement

General movement observation

Practical experience and knowledge of a subject, understanding of people and good observation are pre-requisites for perceptive teaching. Observation improves with practice and experience therefore, young teachers should persevere. It is an exacting and strenuous exercise to observe well, but it gets easier to the point of almost becoming a matter of habit. One can also train oneself to recall what has been seen and re-examine it in detail with hindsight, and this process too improves with practice. Not only must observations be made but there must be a reaction. Some observations are made and used later in the preparation of future lessons, others are acted upon immediately to increase the class's knowledge and skill. There is always this twofold purpose in observing movement. The stored observations should be recorded as soon as possible after lessons, ready for the preparation of the next one. Not only do the recordings help the teacher to be consistent, but the children can witness a plan developing which helps them to understand that there is progression and purpose in their work.

When observation leads to immediate action it may be because the teacher sees some point of interest or need which will help either the class as a whole or an individual. The common need might be for the whole class to feel such things as a full stretch, a rounded shape or a body wave, and if so, the teacher directs the class, all working together to experience whatever is necessary. This should be done at any time in the lesson, both in the floorwork and the apparatus work, whenever it would be of benefit to the class.

General observations also show the standard of movement as a whole and they give the teacher a picture of the movement habits and preferences of individuals. The best opportunities for this type observation are when the class is working freely as in the warming up period at the beginning of the lesson and when the apparatus work first starts. The teacher may sometimes notice when a class is working freely, that they 'infect' one another, so that all may, for example, be working close to the floor and with slow movement. This would be a moment to make them more aware of the enlivening effect of contrasts in movement. They could be challenged to get away from the floor, move high and fast, and discover how this can relate to what they were doing low down and slowly; dynamic and rhythmic changes will be felt and the whole becomes more sensible. Teachers can train themselves to see and sense such problems which easily cause dullness in lessons.

Observation of specific actions
(See Selection and Development, page 145)

The teacher observes the various stages of learning. At the exploratory stage children set to work to explore the task which they have been given, and to discover the possibilities open to them. At this stage the teacher looks first to see if everyone understands the task and how they are trying to carry it out, and deals accordingly with this. Later, the children can be helped individually or as a class to widen their interpretation by being reminded to relate their previous experience to this new situation. Selection and development follow the exploratory stage when a specific skill which the child has discovered or invented, is selected for more intensive practice, or when a new task, based on a sequence of movement relevant to the explorations, may be given. The intention is to clarify the selected action and to gain greater mastery of movement. At this stage the teacher watches individuals, one after another, to find out if there are any common factors which need clarification and if not, provided everyone is working purposefully, attention can be given to a small group or an individual. When such coaching is given it is most necessary for the teacher to stay with the group long enough to see that the teaching is understood and is being carried out. As the skills and sequences take shape, more detailed and analytical observation is needed. As in all movement analysis, the teacher observes the following aspects of action:

The bodily aspect, i e *what* is happening, as a whole and in various parts of the body.

The dynamic aspect, i e *how* speed and energy are used, and the timing, rhythm and flow of the whole.

The spatial aspects, i e *where* the parts of the body are moving in the personal space, and where the body as a whole is going in the general space.

Relationship, i e of partners or groups working together.

161

Bodily aspect

(See Bodily Aspects of Action, page 85)

Participation of the whole body is important for economy and harmony in movement. As the body bends, stretches or twists every part should participate. Children often leave parts of the body inactive and they will, for example, move only the arms and upper part of the body when curling up, and omit to include the legs and lower part of the body in the action. Most children have to be trained to use the trunk effectively in their movements and to move the head in relation to the spine. (Page 104.)

All gymnastic actions are concerned with the management of the body weight, therefore, the teacher must observe how the body is balanced and moved. In locomotion or flight the weight is propelled through space, therefore, the method of propulsion and the way the body is carried must both be observed. In balancing the weight, one must look to see how the weight is brought over the base and balanced on it. To perfect any gymnastic skill one must look not only to how the weight is managed but also to see exactly how the body itself moves, to bring about the action. The teacher may see that actions could be improved by stressing the specific parts of the body such as the legs preparing to receive the weight or the chest lifting to give a sense of elevation in jumping.

Dynamic aspects

(See Dynamic Aspects of Action, page 107)

This aspect becomes most important as soon as the pattern of the action is settled and the child knows how to set about working. The teacher then looks to see if the timing of the action is right, if the climaxes stand out clearly, if the links between phrases are appropriate and if the movement is rhythmical and flowing.

Space aspects

(See Space Aspects of Action, page 126)

What to do and where to go must be worked out in determining the pattern of an action. When apparatus is used angles of approach and retreat as well as the performer's relation to the apparatus are important, e g near or far from it, facing, back or side to it. For clarity of action there must be a definable pattern in space as well as a clear rhythmic pattern. Observing the spatial aspects involves discerning the directions and levels of movement through the general space or in the personal space, or both, and the patterns on the floor and in space which emerge in the performance of specific skills or repeatable sequences of movement.

Relationships
(See Partner and Group Work, page 74)

Only the true relationship of people to each other is being considered here; the wider sense of relationship to inanimate things is not taken into account in this section.

The first point to observe is whether partners or groups have any relationship to each other; there is no point in working together unless this happens. The teacher should notice who takes the lead, and if possible, see that the leadership changes from time to time for it is valuable experience both to lead and be led; but it is difficult for the teacher to step in without interfering and spoiling a group effort. Group work should always involve everyone making a contribution so that all can feel they have had a constructive part to play.

Observation of movement in Partner and Group work should be to discover the point of the action which should always emerge first. All types of matching actions should eventually become identical, therefore the partners may have to adapt their actions if their ability varies greatly. By observing one another, and with the teacher's help, they can achieve both good movement and complete matching. The actions in which partners handle one another need careful observation They can be dangerous unless everyone is prepared and ready, and in the right place. The way the helpers grip, hold, carry and release the performer must be done in a safe way and at the proper moment. The teacher also observes the performer who must be helped to do the right thing at the right time. This may be to hold a shape, or change it, as the situation varies, and generally to move in a way which helps the supporters, and unless specially agreed, the performer must be active and helping, never passive.

The class learns to observe

Children are capable of being acutely observant and the teacher can guide them in many ways and help them to gain experience and understanding of all that can be learnt from pointed observation. They readily learn to be watchful and helpful with one another, and to sense how others may be feeling, and this intuitive way of observation can be developed. The value and desirability of this awareness and such attitudes should frequently be openly appreciated by the teacher. Too many take it all for granted and so lose an opportunity to establish something really worthwhile.

Children are also capable of learning to observe movement more specifically and there should be plenty of opportunity for guided observation in lessons, but care must be taken never to overburden the class with too long or too many observation periods in any one lesson. Breaks in a lesson for observation, must be well planned, quickly and easily organised so that there is no tedious waste of time, and the arrangements must allow for everyone to be able to see from the best angle. This aids concentration. Careful training of classes is needed in order to make the observation interludes work smoothly.

Teaching through observation is a way of 'tuning-in' with a class; classes is needed in order to make the observation interludes work clearly with one another. The teacher presents a way of looking at movement and in turn the youngsters reveal their way of looking and thinking. One way of getting this information is by questioning, and from the responses the teacher learns what sort of guidance is needed both in looking and thinking. Much can also be learnt from the conversations which go on during work; this gives a clue both to interests and understanding!

Partner work can be used at all stages of training observation and incidentally for helping the teacher's work. Partners are paired to check each other's work and, with the teacher's guidance, they give each other help, criticism and verification on various points. The points chosen by the teacher must be crystal clear, and for the inexperienced, should probably be directed to watching parts of the body, such as the head tucked in for a roll or the hips lowered in a landing. As skill increases more subtle points can be stressed such as watching the timing, or the most accented moment in an action, or the rhythm and quality of movement. If observation is to be purposefully and soundly built up, it must be clearly focused. It is often helpful to follow up general observation by work with partners. The general points are made first with the whole class looking and this is followed by working with partners checking each other. One sometimes finds that people who are not physically very able have gifts in helping, and through their skill in observation and constructive criticism they make a valuable contribution and in this way they can gain recognition and prestige. This form of partner work can lead to rapid progress. Frequent short practices of guided observation leads to skill in assessing and criticising movement, and increases understanding. A difficulty for teachers in the diverse activity of educational gymnastics is to give enough help and personal criticism, therefore, by using partners to help each other, this difficulty is somewhat lessened.

Teaching by means of observation has many different purposes such as showing:

A wide range of ideas

Good quality and clarity in movement

Original ideas

Contrasting ways of moving

Technical points

The teacher aims to build up a picture of versatility, liveliness and good quality and, therefore, only what is really worth seeing should be shown.

A wide range of ideas crops up at the exploratory stage and children benefit by seeing each other's work even at this stage. They should not, however, be asked to show anything until they have had time to find one or more solutions to the tasks. A quick way of letting the class see the diversity of 'answers' to tasks is to let half the class work while half watch with the teacher. No detailed looking is asked for and it should be quite clear that the purpose of looking is to see the many and varied ideas which spring from the same source. Classes with enough experience can be asked to comment on the way the demonstrators are using their movement experience and in this way consolidate knowledge previously gained. Leading questions from the teacher may also help to elicit this knowledge. A comprehension of the scope of movement is built up through this type of observation. Observation should always be followed up by action, everyone should work again to try out any new ideas which have inspired them or they may possibly continue with their own inventions, adapting them as a result of what they have seen.

Work of high quality is shown in another way. One child at a time is selected to demonstrate as this enables everyone to concentrate on the points made by the teacher The class must be gathered close to the teacher and in a position where they can see well. The demonstrators are chosen because they have something worthwhile for all to see. This may be a skill or a sequence, or even part of a movement which is supremely well done. The watchers must be guided according to their skill and the less experienced should be given specific points to notice, first how the task has been answered and worked out, and then any points which the teacher was stressing to the class during the learning period. More knowledgeable people can be asked to comment on what they see and one would expect answers connected with the bodily, dynamic or spatial aspects of movement. By seeing well integrated and skilfully performed actions people are helped to recognise the 'rightness' of them. This type of observation must also be clearly focused. While watching perfected skills and sequences there is a special opportunity to stress and draw attention to the quality of movement shown.

Original ideas can be selected for demonstration either by the teacher or by a partner. In the floorwork it is generally quickest to make everyone sit on the floor to watch, and call upon one after another to show their ideas. The teacher or members of the class comment on what they see and the purpose of this observation is also to see a range of ideas. In apparatus work everyone in a section can be asked to show their work, particularly when the teacher has just been coaching them and knows something about each of their actions. The class must come round the apparatus, close enough to see properly. Observation should again be followed up by everyone working with their own ideas, but incorporating in them their new knowledge. Care must be taken not to select original ideas which have no clear purpose but are simply different for the sake of being different. Such actions crop up during the experimental period but they are generally soon rejected, and this is as it should be if the class is also learning to discriminate. Youngsters must learn to judge their own invention and select skills for intensive practice which test them and are worthy of them.

Contrasting ways of interpreting a task can also be selected for showing. In this case three or four people should be asked to demonstrate simultaneously. The demonstrators must be carefully selected so that the point of showing contrasts can be made. These demonstrations can be followed by the rest of the class trying out one or other of the actions they have just seen. This gives everyone an opportunity to experience the feeling of movement composed by someone else and in this way gain an appreciation of movement outside their own range as well as learning respect for the skill of others.

Technical points are probably best demonstrated by the teacher who knows exactly what is required, e g supple, springy footwork, resilient landings, ways of lifting and carrying, or take-off on a springboard. Careful consideration should be given to how and when to demonstrate. Demonstrations should always be of the best quality, and long enough or repeated, so that the class has time to grasp the point. Half-hearted, half-made 'apologetic' demonstrations do more harm than good. An impression of what *is* required must be given, never a negative one of faults. It is often stimulating for a class if the teacher works with them for short periods. Quality of movement can quickly be conveyed in this way, e g light poise in actions with moving and stopping, or calm and smooth stepping actions. Working with a class is sometimes a good way of getting a lagging class started, but it must be done with discretion. The teacher must always be sure that any demonstration made will really prove helpful: a spectacular demonstration can intimidate some people, and classes are put off unless careful judgment is made of when, how, what and why to demonstrate. Demonstrations should always be followed up by the class working and practising the points just made; the value of the observation is largely lost unless practical experience follows immediately.

In selecting children to *demonstrate* it is essential to choose as many different ones as possible and not to use the same demonstrators too often. It is encouraging to be selected to show good or original work, and it is also a means of making the class aware of the variations in the way people move. The teacher must be certain that any child chosen to demonstrate is willing to do so and understands that the choice was made because of the good quality of the work to be shown. No one should ever be asked to demonstrate and then learn that they are showing 'the wrong way'. When this happens it is devastating for most children, and in any case, it is harmful for the rest of the class to be left with an impression of what is not wanted.

It is not only the demonstrators who are important, the observers are too, and the teacher should address them during demonstrations and question them about what they can see and also prove to them how much can be learnt from observation.

All who are watching movement should try to *identify themselves with what they are seeing* and to try and feel inside themselves the movement they are observing. Observation includes sensing, and much can be grasped about movement through empathy. This is a less intellectual way of looking and thinking. Demonstrations should be repeated two or three times so that the observers can get the feeling of what is being done. Generally the teacher comments during the observations, but there are also times when people should be left to absorb in their own way. Observing empathetically helps to develop movement memory as well as building up an appreciation of good movement.

SAFETY AND OBSERVATION

Safety measures are discussed throughout the text and the points made here are a summary to emphasise the relationship of observation to safety in gymnastics. Safety depends to a large extent on the powers of observation of both teacher and children, and also on the ability to act according to what they see. Gymnastics should be spiced with a spirit of adventure and daring, therefore, in common with other robust activities, it must carry some risk. The risks are, however, reduced to an absolute minimum when reasonable precautions are taken. There is no need for special safety training as it should be a continuous process occuring all the time, as the need arises. When children jump they must learn to land with skill, when their balance is upset, they should learn how to cope if they fall and learn ways of recovering equilibrium. The teacher must always be satisfied that no dangerous risks are taken but should not feel that all mistakes need to be averted as these are an essential part of learning.

Some mishaps may be caused by lack of physical skill. These can be practically eliminated by careful grading of work and thorough movement training. The Movement Experience in Part I of lessons develops general awareness of movement and space. This is the part of a gymnastics lesson which particularly should have carry-over value to general skill in all similar situations and to everyday working movements, since it is a development of aptitudes more than a training of specific skills. Quick reactions, lively adaptability, initiative, control of speed and energy in movement, clever use of space and general control of the body are aptitudes which are developed in this part of the lesson, and all these contribute to safety in gymnastics. The teacher constantly observes the stage of skill and ability of the class, and these together with the previous experience are all taken into account in planning lessons. New work is based on these considerations and, therefore, sound progression can be made (see Progression, page 149).

The structure of the lesson and the way it is conducted ensure that there is no excessive strain or fatigue. Young people need plenty of activity and they enjoy hard work if they are led to it in a lively and stimulating way, there is very little danger of overworking a class in a well planned lesson. Many classes come to their lessons from sedentary occupations. The warming up period helps to bridge the gap between inactivity and the active movement of gymnastics in a way which is most suitable for each occasion. The teacher tries to assess the mood of the class in this period, and reacts accordingly. Excited classes may need calming, and reluctant, lethargic classes need gradual rousing and stimulating in ways they will not resist. The warming up period is both a mental and physical preparation for the sharp, keen attention and hard work needed later. Everything in the lesson contributes to greater awareness and efficiency of the body. Strength, resilience, elasticity and suppleness are qualities which can be developed and they give a greater control of the body. Movement 'sense' is gained through varied movement experience, and this gives animal-like skill and ability to assess 'whole' situations and cope with them safely.

The apparatus work is taken in a way which does much to ensure safety. It is more important than ever to follow the policy of self-selected ways of tackling problems in order to avoid unnecessary fear which so often leads to danger. Most children feel intuitively what is right for them, and at least in the first stages, the ways they choose are the ways through which they will most easily learn and gain experience. Children are however generally very trusting and believe that, if the teacher tells them to go ahead and do something, it will be all right. There have been bad accidents where uninitiated children were told they might use trampettes before they had been adequately prepared or were ready for them.

While the children are trying out the apparatus the teacher watches and assesses their needs and how to challenge them in a way which will give scope to everyone. It is important for safety that no one should feel over-pressed since this may make reckless people overstep their ability and timid ones shrink from trying. Challenges should always be to greater *skill in movement* rather than to tests of courage. Courage grows as confidence develops. Some of the chief causes of physical fear in the gymnasium are heights, speed, whirling round, turning upside down and losing balance because these things generate a fear of falling or colliding which may result in pain and damage. Such fears are not readily surmounted by everyone but certain controlled situations may help some to overcome their dreads. Children should be given opportunities to climb as high as they wish on wall bars and window ladders, and swing high on ropes or rings and have a look at the world below them. They can also safely go high by various ways of travelling up inclined forms attached to wall bars or window ladders (rather than bars) because they can be grasped on reaching the top. The experience of gripping and hanging in many ways and by many parts of the body also increases a sense of security. Learning how to share space, travelling fast and stopping suddenly, moving in all directions on many different parts of the body gives people confidence that they themselves, and others, can control what they are doing. Moving with quick, light, nimble movements along or over low apparatus increases body control. Practice in many ways of landing, receiving weight, rolling and transferring weight with agility, takes away some of the fear of falling because people know how to cope when they meet the ground.

Children should not be actively encouraged to jump from big heights before they are skilled enough to manage themselves. Many enjoy jumping down from high places, and if they do so of their own volition, they should only be stopped if the teacher feels that they are not ready for it. Mats must always be used for landing, even from low heights for beginners. It is very difficult to overcome the tension and resistance which is the outcome of jarred feet and bodies. Mats prevent harsh jarring, and when people become really skilful mats will only be needed for landing from apparatus which is higher than forms. (Apart from hygienic reasons, resilient rubber or foam mats are much more satisfactory than fibre mats or cloth-covered agility mattresses. The two latter hurt the feet, toes catch in the cloth, and fibre mats are prickly.)

Spinning on rings or with partners, and rolling along agility mattresses (sideways is easiest for nervous children), eventually overcome the discomfort some people feel when they are whirling around. Some complain, at first, of feeling dizzy, but this is usually overcome through having short turns and plenty of practice. As confidence grows both the distance covered and the speed can be increased. To be able to roll fast is a safety factor; it is often necessary in the recovery after landing. A few children do not like turning upside down or somersaulting round apparatus and they should never be compelled or even over-persuaded. Every sympathetic teacher will be able to find safe and simple ways for them to see the 'world upside down' and there are very few who do not overcome this inhibition.

There are times when people ask for help or for someone to stand by, and then it is necessary to see that the helpers know how to assist. Help should be given in such a way that the performer learns to feel what to do in order to manage alone. Catchers and helpers should never be allowed to drag people over apparatus or forcefully check wild, uncontrolled flight because this hinders the performers from learning how to adjust their weight and manage themselves.

171

Others who need help, may not ask for it but observation will show the teacher whom to assist and when and how to do it. One often sees people giving up, or missing the point of something which has possibility, and this is the moment when the teacher's help is most valuable in giving confidence.

The apparatus work can be taken as Class Activities or as Section Work. Class work makes it easier for the teacher to watch and control the whole class and it is particularly helpful when dealing with inexperienced classes or when introducing new material (page 139). The Section Work is arranged to give varied experience and progression from section to section is planned so that there is no chance of fatiguing the children. The teacher should watch for any signs of fatigue and stop, or change sections in time. Temporary fatigue can be relieved by a very short pause which can be used for giving advice or for observation. Rest periods, sitting down or lying on the floor should not be necessary for a normal healthy group. In fact, yielding suddenly in this way may do more harm than good as the body systems do not very easily respond to such changes. Effort is wasted in getting up and bringing the body back to an efficient working state. In general, the graph of exertion, both mental and physical should rise, throughout the lesson, to a peak in the apparatus work and fall back to normal in the final movements, but within this general pattern there is a rhythmic process of change and contrasting movement so that fatigue, monotony and strain, all possible causes of mishaps, are avoided.

The attitude of both teacher and children and the atmosphere and relationships in the lesson are much more important than any physical precautions taken to ensure safety. There are rarely accidents where the teacher has given full consideration to the choice of work and the class which is to do it, and where the relationship between teacher and class is one of trust, the children knowing they can rely on and feel safe with the teacher, and the teacher, in turn having faith in the children. This depends on contact between them which can only be built up over a period of time. From the earliest stages, however, an attitude of consideration and responsibility for others can be fostered since countless opportunities exist in every lesson to care for the safety of others. It depends on the readiness of everyone to co-operate and use common sense, and these qualities are most likely to be found where the children feel secure and confident. The teacher will notice that many children have plenty of self-confidence. Any child who has led an active, energetic life and climbed trees, jumped from great heights, wrestled, tumbled, rolled and played wild games will not be inhibited in a gymnasium. But the people who have not had such opportunities are sometimes afraid. Physical fears have already been discussed, but there are other fears which at all cost the teacher should try to help people to overcome. Failure, clumsiness and inadequacy can be very frustrating and these negative qualities can check development and make people sullen, unwilling and unco-operative. Such unsure individuals need support and encouragement, help to recognise where their ability lies and assurance that it can be developed, and also that they can contribute in many different ways.

Gymnastic experience can probably make a direct contribution to the safety of children in the daily hazards they encounter, for many accidents in school, at home or on the roads are caused by unalert senses and clumsiness. Lack of observation with eyes, ears and other senses, inattention and slowness of reaction, inability to adapt and failure to judge speed, force and space, incompetence in balance which may cause damaging falls, are all contributory factors. Well trained children should at least have a chance of avoiding some accidents so caused. Through gymnastics they become more aware, alert and observant. To read the statistics of the accidents in the country as a whole is overwhelming and no responsible teacher can remain undisturbed. Physical Education teachers together with teachers of Science, Domestic Science, Woodwork, Metal Work and Craft are in a strong position to combat this devastation. They teach 'dangerous' subjects and are trained to think and anticipate how to take preventive measures. Direct safety rules are a minor part of the measures and even these should be presented in the form of general principles so that they can be obeyed with understanding rather than by blind obedience. But very much more important is the continuous educational process which fosters an ability to assess situations and to think independently, to use initiative and common sense, but most of all to develop attitudes of consideration for others and sympathetic relationship with them.

Index

Main references are given in bold print

Index

176

Index

Books

The Art of Movement and related texts

Effort, Rudolf Laban and F. C. Lawrence, 1947
Mastery of Movement, Rudolf Laban, 2nd edition edit. by Lisa Ullmann, 1960
Modern Educational Dance, Rudolf Laban, 2nd edition edited by Lisa Ullmann, 1963
A Handbook of Modern Dance, Valerie Preston, 1963
Introducing Laban Art of Movement, Betty Redfern, 1965
  (Publisher of all the above—Macdonald and Evans)
Posture and Gesture, Warren Lamb (Gerald Duckworth and Co. Ltd), 1965
Principles of Dance and Movement Notation, Rudolf Laban, 1956
Readers in Kinetography, Laban, Series B, Books I–IV. Valerie Preston, Series C, which includes Gymnastics, is to be published soon. (Publisher —Macdonald and Evans)
Physical Education in the Primary School
  Part I: Moving and Growing, 1952
  Part II: Planning the Programme, 1953
  Prepared by the Ministry of Education and the Central Office of Information
  (Publisher—H.M. Stationery Office)
Educational Gymnastics, Ruth Morison, 1956
Educational Gymnastics for Secondary Schools, Ruth Morison, 1960
Educational Gymnastics. Compiled by the L.C.C. (Publisher—London County Council), 1962
Physical Education in the Primary School, A. Bilborough and P. Jones (Publisher—University of London Press), 1963
Education in Movement (School Gymnastics), W. D. McCameron and P. Pleasance (Publisher—Basil Blackwell, Oxford), 1963
Movement Education for Infants, Compiled by the L.C.C. (Publisher— London County Council), 1964
Teaching Gymnastics, E. Mauldon and J. Layson (Publisher—Macdonald and Evans), 1965
Modern Educational Gymnastics, D. Pallett (Publisher—Pergamon Press), 1965
Childhood and Movement, Diana Jordan (Publisher—Basil Blackwell, Oxford), 1966
Modern Ideas on Physical Education, M. W. Randall (Publisher—G. Bell and Son), 3rd ed., 1967
Education and Physical Education, J. Myrle James (Publisher—G. Bell and Son, London), 1967
Discovery Methods in Physical Education, John Cope (Publisher—Thomas Nelson and Son), 1967

Books

Scientific and other aspects of movement

Quest—A Symposium on Motor Learning—Monograph VI (Published by The National Association for Physical Education of College Women, and the National College Physical Education Association for Men) May 1966. (Obtainable from David C. Bischoff, School of Physical Education, University of Massachusetts, Boyden Hall, Amherst, Massachusetts 01003)

Arnold, P. J., *Education, Physical Education and Personality Development* (Publisher—Heinemann Educational Books Ltd), 1968

Borger, R. and A. E. M. Seaborne, *The Psychology of Learning* (Publisher—Penguin Books Ltd), 1966

Broer, M. R., *Efficiency in Human Movement*, 2nd edition (Publisher—W. B. Saunders and Co., Philadelphia), 1966

Broer, M. R., *An Introduction to Kinesiology* (Publisher—Prentice-Hall Inc.), 1968

Brown, R. C. and Bryant J. Cratty (Editors), *New Perspectives of Man in Action* (Publisher—Prentice-Hall Inc., Englewood Cliffs), 1969

Cratty, J. B., *Movement Behaviour and Motor Learning* (Publisher—Lea and Febinger), 1964

Social Dimensions of Physical Activity (Publisher—Prentice-Hall), 1967

Psychology and Physical Activity (Publisher—Prentice-Hall), 1968

Espenschade, A. S. and Helen M. Eckhert, *Motor Development* (Publisher—Charles E. Merrill Books, Inc., Columbus, Ohio), 1967

Hogg, M. E., *A Biology of Man—Man the Animal*, Volume II (Publisher—Heinemann Educational Books Ltd), 1966

Jacks, L. P., *Education of the Whole Man* (Publisher—University of London Press), 1931

Physical Education (Publisher—Thomas Nelson and Son), 1938

Knapp, B., *Skill in Sport* (Publisher—Routledge and Kegan Paul), 1963

McIntosh, P. C., *Physical Education in England since 1800*, 8th ed. (Publisher—G. Bell and Son), 1968

Miller, S., *The Psychology of Play* (Publisher—Penguin Books), 1968

Metheny, E., *Movement and Meaning* (Publisher—McGraw-Hill, New York), 1968

Munrow, A. D., *Pure and Applied Gymnastics* (Publisher—E. Arnold), 2nd edition, 1963

Roper, R. E., *Movement and Thought* (Publisher—Blackie), 1938

Slusher, H. S., *Man, Sport and Existence: A Critical Analysis* (Publisher—Lea and Febinger, Philadelphia), 1967

Tanner, J. M., *Growth at Adolescence* (Publisher—Basil Blackwell, Oxford), 2nd edition, 1962

Education and Physical Growth (Publisher—University of London Press Ltd), 1961. 4th imp., 1965

Tibble, J. W., *Physical Education and the Educative Process* (University of London Institute of Education: Studies in Education 5) (Publisher—Evans Bros.), 1952

Tricker, R. A. R. and B. J. K., *The Science of Movement* (Publisher—Mills and Boon Ltd., London), 1967

Vendien, C. Lynn and John E. Nixon, Editors, *The World Today in Health Physical Education and Recreation* (Publisher—Prentice-Hall, Inc.), 1968

Vernon, M. D., *The Psychology of Perception* (Publisher—Penguin Books), 1962

Williams, F. J., *Principles of Physical Education* (Publisher—W. B. Saunders and Co., Philadelphia) 8th edition, 1964